International Institute of Business Analysis

Agile Extension to the BABOK® Guide

Version 1.0

D1555912

Table of Contents

Chapter 4:   Agile Techniques   47

Glossary 111

Index 117

Bibliography 121

Contributors 125

Introduction to the Agile Extension

1.1   What is the Agile Extension to the BABOK® Guide?

The *Agile Extension to the BABOK® Guide* describes business analysis areas of knowledge, their associated activities and tasks, and the skills necessary to be effective in their execution within the framework of agile software development.

The purpose of the *Agile Extension to the BABOK® Guide* is to act as a business analysis primer for agile software development approaches and provide business analysis practitioners with:

- an introduction to agile practices for business analysis,
- an overview of business analysis techniques for agile practitioners,
- a set of definitions of typical working practices used by business analysts working on agile projects, and
- an overview of the new and changed roles, skills, and competencies for business analysts.

The *Agile Extension* is of value to business analysts new to agile, as well as those experienced in agile approaches. Both groups, and all those in between, will find helpful information such as an introduction to the practice of business analysis in an agile context, the mapping of existing business analysis techniques to agile practices, and inclusion of techniques that are specific to the practice of business analysis in the agile world.

As the *Agile Extension* highlights, any member of an agile team may engage in the process of business analysis. To that end, each person on an agile team will benefit from having a set of practices and tools from which they can select while working in any one of the different flavors of agile. In the *Agile Extension*, we have called particular attention to the mind-set a business analysis practitioner must have in order to effectively contribute to delivery of ongoing value to stakeholders. We have also described a number of techniques not found in the *BABOK® Guide*, and expanded on others that needed to be described in greater detail. Many of the concepts described here, and the mind-set we describe, will prove valuable to business analysis in any context or environment. Business analysts should always work to ensure that requirements are aligned with organizational goals and objectives and that all stakeholders have a shared understanding of those goals, objectives, and requirements. They must also work to manage risks and validate that the requirements, if delivered, will create real value for stakeholders. Agile approaches can help us find new ways to do these things that support continuous delivery of working software, but the responsibility to do these things is inherent to the profession of business analysis.

1.2   What is Agile?

Agile is a term used to describe a number of iterative development approaches that have developed over time. Agile originated within the world of software development. However, with its success and ability to adapt to individual contexts and environments, agile has evolved into being utilized by non-software related projects.

The term agile can have many different interpretations. It is the Agile Manifesto (www.agilemanifesto.org) that clearly defines what agile means, and the principles that support it.

Manifesto for Agile Software Development

We are uncovering better ways of developing software by doing it and helping others do it. Through this work we have come to value:

Individuals and interactions over processes and tools

Working software over comprehensive documentation

Customer collaboration over contract negotiation

Responding to change over following a plan

That is, while there is value in the items on the right, we value the items on the left more.

Principles Behind the Agile Manifesto

We follow these principles:

1. Our highest priority is to satisfy the customer through early and continuous delivery of valuable software.

2. Welcome changing requirements, even late in development. Agile processes harness change for the customer's competitive advantage.

3. Deliver working software frequently, from a couple of weeks to a couple of months, with a preference to the shorter timescale.

4. Business people and developers must work together daily throughout the project.

5. Build projects around motivated individuals. Give them the environment and support they need, and trust them to get the job done.

6. The most efficient and effective method of conveying information to and within a development team is face-to-face conversation.

7. Working software is the primary measure of progress.

8. Agile processes promote sustainable development. The sponsors, developers, and users should be able to maintain a constant pace indefinitely.

9. Continuous attention to technical excellence and good design enhances agility.

10. Simplicity--the art of maximizing the amount of work not done--is essential.

11. The best architectures, requirements, and designs emerge from self-organizing teams.

12. At regular intervals, the team reflects on how to become more effective, then tunes and adjusts its behavior accordingly.

For the purposes of the *Agile Extension to the BABOK® Guide*, we characterize the Manifesto and its Principles as a philosophy and an approach.

The Agile Manifesto uses the term developers to describe the team who works on building the product. This is a cross-functional team of skilled individuals who bring a variety of expertise to bear on the process of building a software product. The skills that developers require to do this include business analysis, technical design, programming in various languages and tools, testing, UI design, technical writing, architecture, and whatever else is needed to produce working software. Working software is a product which is in the production environment delivering value for our customers.

1.3   What does Agile Mean for Business Analysis?

Much like other approaches, business analysis is central to the success of agile projects. Business analysis is necessary to enable a diverse group of customers to speak with a single voice. Not all agile projects have the defined role of business analyst, but all agile projects do practice business analysis. Business analysis may be done by one or more members of an agile team.

In the agile world, software requirements are developed through continual exploration of the business need. Requirements are elicited and refined through an iterative process of planning, defining acceptance criteria, prioritizing, developing, and reviewing the results. Throughout the iterative planning and analysis of requirements, business analysis practitioners must constantly ensure that the features requested by the users align with the product's business goals, especially as the business goals evolve and change over time. This is true for new software development, maintenance of existing software, migration of software and data, or implementation of commercial off-the-shelf (COTS) software. It applies to very large mission-critical software projects in heavily regulated industries, as well as to development of small or simple software functionality in unregulated environments. Agile business analysis is primarily about increasing the delivery of business value to the sponsors and customers of the project/product being developed. Agile business analysis aligns with the values and principles of the Agile Manifesto (www.agilemanifesto.org):

- We value individuals and interactions over processes and tools.
- Our highest priority is to satisfy our customer through early and continuous delivery of valuable software.
- Working software is the primary measure of progress.

Agile business analysis is about ensuring the right information is available to the development team in the right level of detail, at the right time, so they can build the right product.

The techniques of business analysis do not change dramatically in the agile environment. However, the timing and how they are used do change. Artifacts such as personas, data models, use cases, story maps, and business rules continue to be employed, but are kept as lightweight as possible. Artifacts that are more quickly developed such as diagrams, maps, and lists tend to provide more value to an agile project than highly detailed specifications that slow down the development of working software. Lower-fidelity artifacts are developed for the sole purpose of building the software for a specific iteration and only need to be intelligible to the team during the course of the iteration. Long-lived artifacts, on the other hand, are intended to be utilized beyond the scope of development. Long-lived artifacts may include the business case, charter, and documentation that is used to communicate what the software does and why it does it.

Agile offers the opportunity for business analysis to benefit from the frequent feedback provided by the business. By reviewing the results of successive iterations with the business stakeholders, analysts have the opportunity to

- refine the product's requirements to ensure they maintain cohesion with the business needs for the product,
- identify and mitigate risk early in the project, and
- ensure that the right solution is delivered.

Whenever possible, in agile projects, high risk items are addressed in early iterations. This allows the team to mitigate issues and the possible rework required if risk items are not addressed until later in the project. Facilitating risk discovery and assisting the team in remaining focused on effective risk mitigation is central to the analyst's role on an agile team.

Iterative development processes provide opportunities for increased efficiencies in the practice of business analysis. In plan-driven projects, requirements are developed in their entirety prior to the development phase. As risk elements are uncovered and business needs evolve, certain requirements may change or be eliminated outright; making the work effort put into those requirements wasted. By providing just-in-time requirements, there is less rework of requirements because only the requirements required for the current release are defined in detail and developed.

1.4   What does Agile Mean for Business Analysts?

The early stages of agile's evolution frequently relied on a single individual being able to make all the decisions regarding the development of the software. As agile projects grow in size and breadth, and become adopted by larger and more diverse organizations, the role of business analyst has become a vital contributor. Business analysis skills are needed to elicit and analyze the needs and wishes of diverse stakeholders and for arriving at a single, agreed upon product vision.

In some projects a dedicated business analyst role is unnecessary. This is not to say that business analysis is not conducted during the course of the project, only that it may be done by any member, or members, of the overall development team.

There are a variety of ways a business analyst can be engaged on an agile project:

- The analyst might be the facilitator in more complex environments, bringing divergent business stakeholders together and helping them speak with a single voice so the project team is not confused by contradictory and conflicting perspectives.
- The analyst might act as the product owner/customer representative where they are empowered by the business to make decisions on product features and priority.
- The analyst could act as a surrogate product owner, in situations where the business product owner is not available.
- The analyst might act as the second in command to a business product owner with limited availability.
- The analyst could take the role of coach in an environment where the business product owner is competent and committed, but has limited IT project experience and the rest of the development team are lacking in domain knowledge.
- The analyst can play a central role in defining and communicating the acceptance criteria prior to development work commencing.
- The analyst can be involved in creating and executing acceptance tests.
- The analyst can ensure that the team remains focus on the business value of the project.
- The analyst can play a role in identifying important requirements that might not have been actively represented by stakeholders.

Irrespective of job titles, business analysis is about ensuring the project is able to deliver the maximum value for customers and adapting to the evolving business needs.

The techniques utilized in agile approaches do not represent a major shift for business analysts. They continue to utilize many of the tools and techniques defined in *A Guide to the Business Analysis Body of Knowledge®* (*BABOK® Guide*). What has changed is the timing and the usage of these techniques. The rigors and demands of agile projects also require business analysts to utilize and develop skills that they may not have previously exercised at a high level. In an agile environment, the success of the business analyst relies increasingly on such interpersonal skills as communication, facilitation, coaching and negotiation. These skills are certainly central to the success of an analyst in any environment. However, due to the inter-connectedness of agile teams, if these skills are not being effectively utilized, the number of requests that can be adequately understood and prioritized decreases. This results in fewer items making it into the solution implementation for a given release.

Analysts are required to approach requirements from a 360 degree perspective. They are required to work with the business sponsor on a strategic level, and define how the proposed product or feature aligns with the organization's portfolio and strategy. They must then work with the business and project team to break this vision down into requirements that support effective and accurate estimation. In an agile project this is done for each iterative release, as opposed to the single requirements phase that exists in plan-driven approaches. The analyst delivers just-in-time, detailed requirements to the development team so they can build only what is required for a specific iteration.

Business analysts play a key role in facilitating a shared understanding of the business need for the project with all stakeholders. It is the role of the business analyst to facilitate a shared, agreed upon vision for the product across the entire delivery team. Understanding and presenting multiple view points, alongside the ability to hold successful conversations, trump the need for formal, detailed, long term artifacts such as requirement documents.

One of the key elements for a business analyst working in an agile environment is the ability to use feedback to drive change. It is incumbent on the analyst to constantly review requirements with the business stakeholders and ensure that any shifts in business needs are accurately reflected in future releases of the product.

1.5   What makes a BA Successful on an Agile Team?

The very nature of agile approaches requires all team members to be operating at a very high level of competency, skill, and effectiveness. This is especially true for business analysts. On successful agile teams, business analysts are an integral component of the delivery team. They are active participants, if not the actual facilitators of planning, analyzing, testing, and demonstrating activities.

The business analyst plays a central role in ensuring that the product road map clearly defines the product's strategic alignment to the business need. The analyst holds shared responsibility in defining the strategic criteria for completion of the project. This requires the analyst to exercise an extremely high level of skill in communication, facilitation, and negotiation. They require the ability to listen to and understand feedback from all stakeholders and use this feedback to drive the changes required to the requirements and priorities of the project.

Business Analysis in Agile Approaches

Agile is a term used to describe a number of iterative development approaches that have developed over time. It is important to note that though most agile approaches are iterative, not all iterative approaches are agile. Common traits amongst agile approaches include frequent product releases, high levels of real-time collaboration within the project team and with customers, reduced time intensive documentation, and regular, recurring assessments of value and risk to allow for change.

A few examples of agile approaches include

- Scrum,
- Extreme Programming (XP),
- Kanban,
- Crystal,
- Dynamic Systems Development Method (DSDM),
- Agile Unified Process (AUP),
- Feature Driven Development, and
- Adaptive Software Development.

Each agile approach has its own unique set of characteristics that allow teams to select an approach that best suits the project at hand. It is common for project teams to blend characteristics from more than one agile approach based on unique team composition, skills, experience, operating environment, and other factors. Due to time and space limitations the *Agile Extension* does not provide comprehensive information on each approach. We do provide an overview of Scrum, Extreme Programming (XP), and Kanban in order to provide a level of context for those who are not familiar with these agile approaches.

Agile approaches tend to focus on achieving business value based on business needs. Plan-driven approaches tend to focus on achievement of their quality/ cost/delivery analysis (QCD) within the project life-cycle. When working in an agile environment business analysts work to transform business need into business value.

Although we do use the plan-driven approach as a means of articulating some of the differentiating aspects of agile approaches, it should be noted that these are not the only approaches available to those practicing business analysis. The *Agile Extension to the BABOK® Guide* does not recommend one approach over another, nor does it take a position on the benefits of applying agile approaches. Due diligence and research is required when selecting an approach.

2.1 Scrum

Scrum is one of the most predominant agile process frameworks in use today. In the Scrum framework work on a project is performed in a series of iterations, called sprints, which generally last from 2 to 4 weeks. At the end of each sprint, the team must produce working software of a high enough quality that it could potentially be shipped or otherwise delivered to a customer.

Within the Scrum framework there are four formal meetings, known as ceremonies:

- sprint planning,
- the daily scrum (or stand-up),
- sprint reviews, and
- sprint retrospectives.

2.1.1 Backlogs

In the Scrum framework, a product backlog lists the requirements for an iteration prioritized by highest customer value. The backlog is a collection of user stories that include the expected business value. The user stories are refined as the acceptance criteria is developed. As the team collaborates with the customer for the project, the product backlog is updated with each request.

The product backlog is constantly prioritized, such that at any given time it can be used to identify high priority requests for the solution being developed. At the beginning of each sprint, in the sprint planning ceremony, the team reviews the prioritized product backlog and identifies the customer's highest-priority user stories that can be completed within the sprint period. The selected stories are then placed on a smaller sprint backlog.

2.1.2 Sprint Planning and Execution

During the sprint the team refines their understanding of the selected user stories and works to ensure that they are completed within the defined time limit of the sprint. As sprints are executed, the team meets once per day (referred to as the daily scrum or stand-up meeting) to briefly discuss what they are working on and identify any impediments that may prevent them from completing their work. At the end of the sprint, the team delivers working and tested software that fully implements the sprint's user stories. The sprint is then completed with a customer review and a retrospective. During the customer review, the software is demonstrated and the customer provides feedback. During the retrospective, the team meets and collaborates to find ways to improve both the product and their processes used to deliver the product. Both the customer review and the retrospective may identify additional items that feed into the product backlog. These items are then used to re-prioritize the product backlog for the next sprint planning session.

The following illustration demonstrates a typical scrum life-cycle.

FIGURE 2.1 Scrum Life-cycle

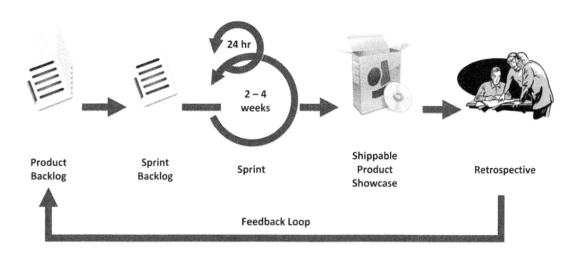

2.1.3   Roles and Responsibilities

In Scrum, there are three roles:

- **Product Owner**: The product owner provides the overall vision and direction of the product. They are responsible for defining the product backlog and perform backlog prioritization according to customer value.
- **Scrum Master**: The scrum master ensures the team's Scrum processes are followed and the team functions well through collaboration and facilitation. They manage any impediments that may prevent the team from accomplishing work and shield the team from external interferences.
- **The Team**: The team is responsible for developing and delivering the product. They collaborate with the product owner to determine what user stories will be delivered in a sprint and commit to delivery of the user stories.

2.1.4   Business Analysis in Scrum

While Scrum focuses on value driven development it does not address business analysis activities in detail and many of these activities occur as implicit steps in the scrum framework. The following illustration shows the typical scrum life cycle with business analysis techniques superimposed.

FIGURE 2.2 Business Analysis in Scrum

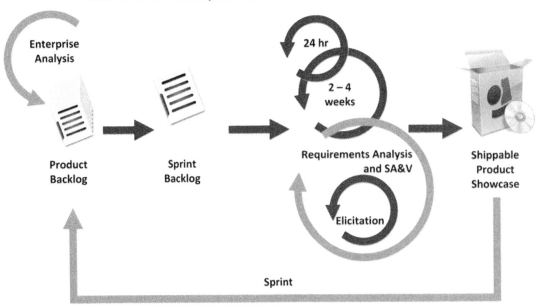

The product backlog is built through a combination of enterprise analysis work (identifying gaps and new capabilities required to accomplish organizational goals and defining their value to the organization) and solution assessment and validation (identifying ways in which the existing solution can be enhanced to better deliver business value). Within a sprint, business analysis activities focus on eliciting the requirements for the sprint backlog items being worked and the acceptance criteria for those items. This approach is frequently referred to as just-in-time requirements elicitation; developing only what is required for the current sprint and only done to the level of detail required to enable the team to build the product and acceptance criteria.

2.1.5   Techniques

- **Backlog Management**: Backlog management is the primary method of handling both requirements prioritization and change management in most agile approaches.
- **Retrospectives**: Retrospectives are a common practice used by agile teams seeking to improve their ways of working. Business analysts should look for feedback on the requirements they provide to the team and how and when those requirements are provided in order to find ways to improve their processes.
- **MoSCoW Prioritization**: MoSCoW Prioritization is used to prioritize stories (or other elements). MoSCoW provides a way to reach a common understanding on relative importance of delivering a story or other piece of business value in the product.

2.2   Extreme Programming (XP)

Extreme Programing (XP) began being used by development teams in the mid-1990s. Like other agile approaches, XP is iterative in nature and provides small releases at the end of each iteration. XP's primary focus is on the engineering aspects of agile software development and is based on 12 practices in four categories.

TABLE 2.1 Extreme Programming Categories

	XP Categories			
	Fine Scale Feedback	**Continuous Process**	**Shared Understanding**	**Programmer Welfare**
XP Practices	• Pair Programming • Planning Game • Test Driven Development • Whole Team Testing	• Continuous Integration • Re-factoring • Small Releases • Coding Standards	• Collective Code Ownership • Simple Design • System Metaphor	• Sustainable Pace

2.2.1 User Stories

XP uses the concept of user stories as a central mechanism to define requirements. They are created by users of the system to define features and functionality to be included in the solution and do not contain a high level of detail. Each user story is normally accompanied by a list of acceptance criteria which identify specific details about the story.

Stories are used to:

- prioritize work into iterations,
- identify risk associated with a request,
- estimate the effort required to deliver the request, and
- establish a conversation between the team and the product owner around the subject of the real business need, in order to confirm a common understanding of what has to be done.

2.2.2 Release Planning and Execution

XP relies on three levels of planning:

- release planning,
- iteration planning, and
- daily planning.

Release planning identifies the next set of usable features that could make up a release. There are often several iterations worth of work before the product is release-ready. Iteration planning serves to plan each incremental iteration that will ultimately result in a releasable product. Finally, in daily planning the team plans out each day's activities to ensure the team is on schedule and identify risks that may have arisen.

In XP, release plans are used to track and describe what features or functionality is to be delivered in each product release. The release plan is similar to the concept of the product backlog in the Scrum framework. Iteration planning meetings are then used as a vehicle for team collaboration in planning the coming iteration. As the team works to schedule the release, the user stories are ordered based on the most important features to the customer, ensuring that the most important features are always delivered first. Stories are decomposed into their granular functional requirements in a technique known as story decomposition, on a just-in-time basis. Then, through story elaboration, the team identifies the detailed design and acceptance criteria for the story.

While an iteration is underway, XP is also similar to Scrum in that it utilizes daily meetings as the key communication vehicle for the team. This daily stand-up meeting is used to facilitate daily planning activities and review progress since the prior day's stand-up. In practice, teams employing the XP approach frequently combine such elements as cadence, roles, and ceremonies (such as sprint planning and sprint reviews) from the Scrum framework.

The following diagram provides an overview of the XP model.

FIGURE 2.3 **Extreme Programming Model**

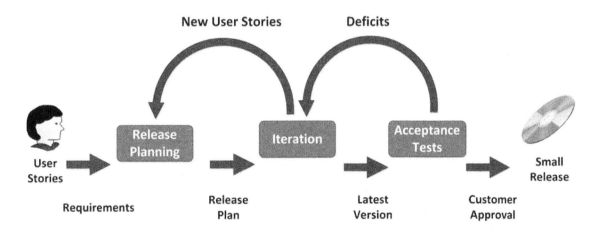

2.2.3   Roles and Responsibilities

In Extreme Programing there are four key roles:

- **Customer**: The customer creates and prioritizes the user stories and performs risk analysis.
- **Developer**: The developer communicates directly with the customer and builds only what is necessary to deliver on each iteration.
- **Tracker**: The tracker keeps track of the schedule and the metrics.
- **Coach**: The coach guides and mentors the team in applying XP practices effectively.

2.2.4   Business Analysis in XP

While XP does focus on value-driven development, it does not explicitly address business analysis activities. XP relies on the fundamental assumption that the customer role is filled by a small number of people who know what the most valuable features will be. When XP is applied at a larger scale, or with customers who do not have a clear vision of the incremental value of features, a business analyst adds significant value in facilitating and negotiating with stakeholders to reach a shared understanding of what the most valuable deliverables will be. A business analyst can also contribute by facilitating story mapping.

In traditional XP, the user stories are created and managed directly by the customer. This can lead to unfiltered requirements that are at risk of constraining a solution without consideration for root cause or applicability to other customer groups. Business analysis skills can be used to ensure underlying problems are being addressed in a way that works for most, if not all, of the stakeholders on the project, as well as ensure thorough acceptance criteria have been collected for each user story. On projects where there is a dedicated business analyst they often perform story decomposition and elaboration activities.

2.2.5   Techniques

- **User Story**: User stories identify which roles in the story provide value and therefore identifies the stakeholders who can elaborate on that value.

- **Story Mapping**: Story maps show relationships between user stories and larger activities that the user must be able to accomplish.
- **Story Decomposition**: Epics, features, or minimally marketable features (MMF) tie groups of user stories together into larger packages that can be discussed with stakeholders.
- **Story Elaboration**: Defines the detailed design and acceptance criteria for a user story on a just-in-time / just-enough basis.

2.3   Kanban

Scrum and XP are frameworks that define sets of roles, ceremonies, and practices for product delivery. In the context of software development, Kanban is an approach for managing the flow of work to allow for evolutionary change. With roots in the Theory of Constraints and Lean product development, Kanban has five key principles:

- visualize the work,
- limit work in process,
- focus on flow,
- make process policies explicit, and
- continually improve.

Unlike the other agile frameworks that we have discussed, Kanban development does not require fixed iterations. Work moves through the development process as a continuous flow of activity. A key feature of Kanban is to limit the amount of work underway at any one time (referred to as the Work in Progress Limit or WIP). In this approach the team works only on a fixed number of items at any one time and work may begin on a new item only when it is required to maintain flow downstream and after the previous item has been completed.

2.3.1   Queues

Kanban relies on the use of work queues to manage the flow of activities that must take place to deliver a working product. The format and content for work queues is less prescriptive in this approach than others we have looked at. The queue should only describe the work to be completed in relative priority to deliver the product. For this reason, the Kanban approach is often combined with approaches such as Scrum where the backlog is used as the implementation for the queue. When a new feature request is received, it is assessed for relative priority and urgency and then placed into the queue in its relative position, maintaining the order by priority.

Analogous to the Scrum technique of managing the product backlog, the team evaluates the features waiting in the input queue to see if they are too large or out of scope for the upcoming release. For items that are too large to be completed before a planned release date, the project team will break the item down (decompose it) into smaller chunks of work, deciding which will be included in the release and which will not. The team then reassesses the priority of the items in the queue and reorders them as needed to maintain a continuous, prioritized flow of work.

2.3.2   Roles and Responsibilities

Kanban does not include defined, mandated roles or business analysis practices. Like any agile approach, it strives to break down work such that individual work items can be implemented in a relatively short period of time. The Kanban approach also attempts to bring the project team together by increasing communication and collaboration, enabling the team to work together as a collective and cohesive unit.

2.3.3   Business Analysis in Kanban

Business analysis, like all activities in the Kanban approach, occurs in a constant and continuous flow through the life of a project. In order to maintain a prioritized queue of work business analysis techniques are used to elicit new product features. Requirements analysis practices are then used to prioritize the requirements based on business value, while also continuously using business analysis techniques for scoping the product and managing the queue of requirements.

When planning and managing tasks in the Kanban approach, Service Level Agreements (SLAs) are used to maintain the estimates for how long a feature or chunk of work will take to be completed. In Kanban, this estimate includes the planning and analysis activities that take place before software development begins. This approach forces a business analyst to focus on planning and monitoring activities, enabling constant revision and refinement of estimates as each new request enters the analysis portion of the cycle. In a Kanban project, the business analyst only begins to define requirements for a new work item when the queue steps forward. At that point the development team begins to work on one of the completed requirements while the business analyst begins collecting requirements for the next item in the queue. By openly and visibly managing the work of the project team, inefficiencies will surface as process improvement opportunities. This will help to mitigate the risk related to the timing of business analysis activities, enabling the business analyst to manage the risk early in the process.

2.4 Levels of Planning in Agile Approaches

Due to the fluid, dynamic nature of agile approaches, it is important to understand when and how to apply different planning techniques and the appropriate level of detail for each level of planning. It is important to note that many of the techniques used in an agile environment are similar to traditional techniques; what is different is how and when these techniques are applied. Just-in-time and just enough requirements that are consistently validated by the business are central to the analyst's role in agile approaches.

When undergoing planning exercises in the agile world, it is helpful to consider how the analyst's role differs from plan-driven development approaches. In agile the role of the analyst is central to the value of the project. The analyst holds a key role in maximizing value by facilitating the interactions with all the project stakeholders. Exceptionally high communication, facilitation, and negotiation skills are an important set of tools for analysts in the agile environment.

Successful agile projects follow a consistent planning cadence of

- strategy,
- release,
- iteration,
- daily, and
- continuous.

Through this cadence, the requirements for the project are progressively elaborated to an appropriate level of detail. At each step stable concepts are captured, context is captured, and learning opportunities are identified. One of the key tenets of agile is to perform a sufficient level of analysis at each planning level. Too much analysis up front can result in the creation of documents that are subject to change, require the business user to explain their needs multiple times, and may not be necessary to achieve the goals of the project. Too little analysis up front can result in irresponsible commitments, rework, and a lack of focus on customer value. Most agile teams focus on daily work, iteration, and release planning.

FIGURE 2.4 **Agile Levels of Planning**

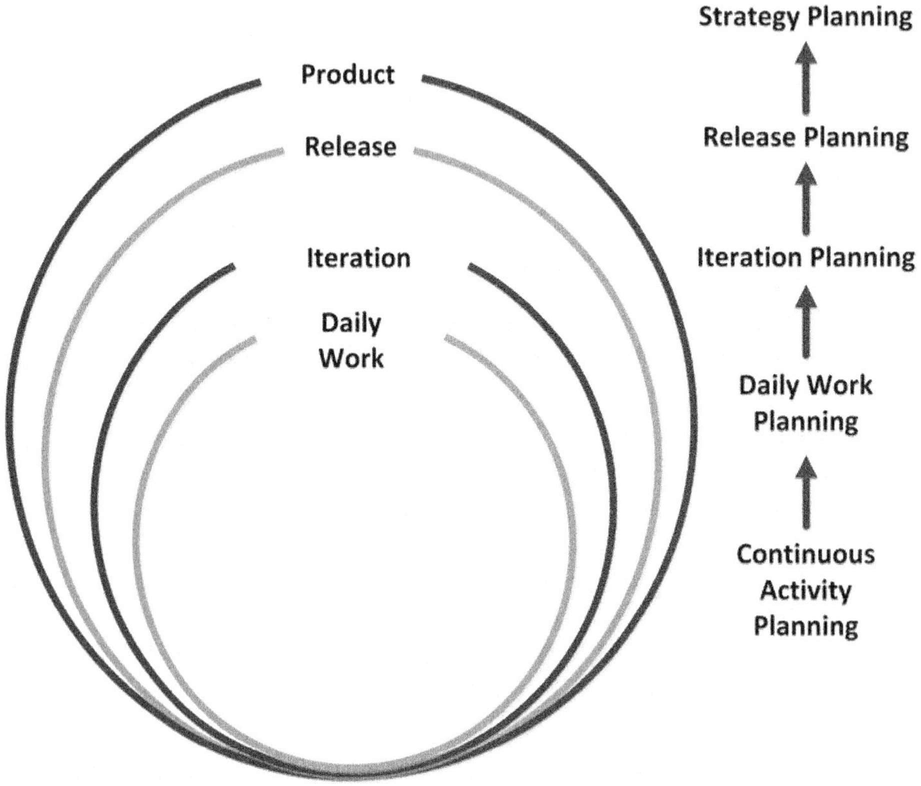

2.4.1   Strategy Planning

Projects and product development efforts start with a vision of the business direction or need. The vision includes the what, why, and success criteria for the effort. The vision is often associated with a roadmap. The roadmap includes the high-level scope and may include an initial architecture. In addition to activities such as establishing a vision, scope, and roadmap, the strategy work on an agile project includes the initial creation of a feature request list. For example, in Scrum this entails seeding the initial requests in a product backlog or, in XP, user stories. This is analogous to pre-project elicitation of basic stakeholder requirements that are used to facilitate discussions on scoping and phasing in plan-driven projects.

At a strategic level, the person who owns the product or is leading the initiative helps the delivery team to

- identify the desired business value,
- define the business context,
- define the context of the solution needed,
- identify and outlines the steps to realize the vision with the delivery team,
- identify the principles which should be used when prioritizing work, and
- define the product roadmap.

Strong enterprise business analysis skills are required to effectively plan a strategy for an agile project. In some ways, you could argue that these skills become more important in agile approaches. This is because without direction based on business value and a clearly defined scope and audience, agile projects are at risk for delivering incremental features that never come together to create end-to-end value for any one customer group. Without a roadmap and success criteria for the product, agile projects could conceivably go on forever, wasting time, money, and other resources in the process.

2.4.2   Release Planning

Release planning is the activity in which the person who owns the product groups activities and allocates them to teams. Teams work on defining enough detail to responsibly commit to some range of scope for the release. When considering release, teams consider business conditions and operational readiness. Teams should release when the benefits of delivery outweigh the costs associated with release. The release is defined by a date, strategic theme, and planned feature set. Release dates can be linked to events, like conferences or compliance requirements. In release planning the target scope is agreed upon and the prioritized list of feature requests, such as a product backlog, is used as the basis for planning.

2.4.3   Iteration Planning

Many agile teams work in fixed time windows called sprints or iterations. An iteration planning event is held at, or shortly before, the start of each iteration. Prior to that iteration planning meeting, the items in the feature request list that are being considered for the iteration need to be sufficiently understood, thus enabling the team to responsibly make a commitment. In Scrum this is known as grooming the backlog. In continuous flow models like Kanban, the feature request list is still groomed before it is committed, but the planning cadence is based on demand, not on a defined time period. On some teams, the customer or owner of the product collaborates with the delivery team to groom the request list prior to iteration planning, while other teams use low-fidelity specifications developed during workshops held prior to iteration planning. This work is comprised of requirement communication and analysis, with additional elicitation and documentation as needed.

In iteration planning the work that will be performed in the sprint is identified, estimated, reviewed, and committed to be completed. The delivery team meets with the customer or the owner of the product to understand the requirements and acceptance criteria, and to gain clarity on specifications. This is analogous to the work in a plan-driven project where the business analyst communicates requirements to stakeholders. At the end of iteration planning, the delivery team commits to delivering an increment of working, tested, and deployable code.

After an iteration has been completed an iteration review or product demonstration is held. The results of the product demonstration feed into the next cycle of iteration planning. The product demonstration meeting is similar to light-weight user acceptance testing and is generally limited to a maximum of 4 hours.

During the product demonstration

- the delivery team demonstrates how the code that was developed meets the acceptance criteria,
- the owner of the product determines which items on the feature list have been completed in the iteration,
- any new requests that arise from the customer as a result of viewing the latest product are added to the feature request list, and
- the owner of the product and delivery team review the state of the business, the market, and the technology, and re-prioritize the feature request list for the next iteration.

After the iteration review meeting the process starts up again. While a working product is the expected output of each iteration, many agile teams will wait to release a product until several iterations worth of work have been completed. The team must determine the appropriate trade-off point between the cost to deliver the latest product and the amount of new or improved functionality that will be delivered to the customer base. Iterations proceed until enough features have been done to complete or release a product.

2.4.4 Daily Work Planning

Many agile teams perform daily team meetings to coordinate the work. The daily meeting is usually a fifteen minute meeting designed to clarify the state of the work.

During the daily meeting the team

- gets a global snapshot of the project,
- discovers any new dependencies,
- addresses any personal needs of committed individuals, and
- adjusts the work plan to meet the needs of the day and ensure the team can deliver on the iteration commitment.

Frequently the dialogue held during this meeting uncovers items that lack clarity or require further analysis. The team then identifies a plan for dealing with these impediments to the project. This often entails assigning someone to do further business analysis work for elicitation and analysis on the impacted requirements.

2.4.5 Continuous Activity Planning

There are many dynamic activities, efforts, and challenges that arise during the planning activities of agile projects.

Here are some guiding principles that those conducting business analysis may find helpful:

- Start with value and keep the team true to value. It is vital that the individual holding the business analysis role is paying close attention to the project's business value.
- Low-fidelity artifacts serve as an enabler of business value by creating context and generating shared understanding. However, they do not replace, or even take precedence over effective collaboration and conversation.
- Business analysis is about facilitating discussion and understanding. Business analysts may not possess the depth of

understanding about the business as does the business sponsor, or as much about technology as the technology team.

- Operate in the best interest of the business over time. Responsibly balance value and capacity to deliver.

- Identify and communicate competing concerns and gaps in understanding between the business and technology. Ensure that common understanding is reached.

- Resources are limited and valuable. Always assist in maximizing value over time.

- Assist the team to take action. Effectively communicate what is required when taking the next steps. Ensure that feedback is clearly understood and acted on by the team.

- Deliver incrementally and iteratively. Do the smallest, simplest thing that could possibly work. Iterate to reach minimal value. Progressively elaborate in small pieces while testing assumptions and articulating clear acceptance criteria.

- Produce the smallest amount of documentation that meets the needs of the team and deliver it just in time.

Mapping Agile Techniques to the BABOK® Guide

The following areas of knowledge represent a selection of popular agile business analysis techniques identified through the development of the *Agile Extension to the BABOK® Guide*. Many of the business analysis techniques described in the *BABOK® Guide* continue to be usable in an agile context. In addition, there may also be other techniques not listed here or in the *BABOK® Guide* that may prove to be useful and applicable in a particular situation. Techniques not listed in the *Agile Extension to the BABOK® Guide* should not be discredited as valuable in the context of performing agile business analysis.

In the following section we focus our attention on common business analysis techniques applicable to agile that are supplemental to those described in the *BABOK® Guide.* The agile techniques that are mapped to *BABOK®* Knowledge Areas in this chapter are explained in greater detail in Chapter 4: Techniques.

3.1 Business Analysis Planning and Monitoring

Business Analysis Planning and Monitoring (Chapter 2 of the *BABOK® Guide*) describes the work required for a business analyst to determine the activities that will be required to perform business analysis through the life cycle of a product. In agile approaches, business analysis planning can be done up-front or deferred until work on an activity is ready to begin. Some business analysts will develop an initial plan, which gets updated prior to starting each new activity to account for change and ensure the plan is always up to date.

3.1.1 Plan Business Analysis Approach (*2.1*)

Agile approaches fall into the general category of change-driven approaches as described in the *BABOK® Guide*. Some business analysis work will generally be performed up front to define a vision for the project and how the problem or opportunity will be addressed, but detailed analysis will be performed as-needed. If the problems the software is supposed to solve are unclear, or several stakeholder groups have conflicting interests, it may be necessary to do business analysis work prior to the beginning of a project. That up-front analysis will provide a better understanding of underlying problems, their drivers, and the goals of the stakeholders in order to reach agreement on the vision for the product. This includes a shared agreement on the problem or opportunity the product is intended to address. As a result, there may be planned business analysis activities that are defined in the pre-project phase, in addition to the business analysis activities that are defined for each cycle of work, such as for an iteration.

.1 Agile Techniques

- **Backlog Management**: Backlog management is the primary method of handling requirements planning, prioritization, and change management in most agile approaches. Because the backlog often describes the breakdown of requirements in the relative order in which the features should be implemented, it can serve as a description for the order in which business analysis activities will take place. Some backlogs also include business analysis activities as tasks to be completed in a development cycle.

- **Planning Workshop**: Business analysts participate in planning workshops to determine the business analysis effort and activities to support a team objective.

- **Real Options**: Real option analysis may help determine when business analysis needs to be conducted to investigate a particular business issue.

- **Retrospectives**: The feedback from prior retrospectives should be considered when selecting the approach.

3.1.2   Conduct Stakeholder Analysis (2.2)

Stakeholders may be challenged by the rapid, iterative development found in an agile project and the need to be on call whenever information is needed by the team. In agile development, business analysts need to consider the impact of the agile cadence on the stakeholder and how things like progress elaboration will affect expectations. Business analysts need ask questions such as, can the stakeholder participate in updating the processes, interactions, and product specifications during the course of the project? Prototyping and frequent feedback from stakeholders can help to refine what is known about the needs of a stakeholder or stakeholder group

.1 Agile Techniques

- **Collaborative Games**: Many collaborative games can be used to understand the perspectives of various stakeholder groups.
- **Personas**: Personas can help the analyst or development team by enabling them to better describe and visualize the needs of a group or archetype of stakeholders, understanding how the archetype will derive value from a solution, potential risks for the archetype, and other information that will help the team to better understand the needs of the stakeholder groups involved with the project.

3.1.3   Plan Business Analysis Activities (2.3)

Business analysis activities are planned as needed, usually at the start of the project and refined with each iteration or when a new work item is ready for analysis. The business analyst should always be aware of and prepared to address the next iteration of work, keeping the vision for the product and evolution of incremental value in mind. There is less of a focus on formal documentation (although it still can be required to meet statutory or regulatory requirements, or to capture knowledge developed during the analysis and development process) and more focus on progressive elaboration of documentation throughout the life of the project. Also, much of the elaboration is replaced by interactions and ceremony so these outcomes need to be accomplished with activities addressed in the communication plan.

.1 Agile Techniques

- **Planning Workshop**: Decisions regarding business analysis activities will usually be made during a planning workshop.

3.1.4   Plan Business Analysis Communication (2.4)

During development, formal communication of requirements is generally replaced with ad-hoc informal discussions and modeling. Some deliverables are replaced by specific interactions or ceremonies. By definition, these interactions and ceremonies require real-time participation by the business analyst. Formal documentation may be developed following development of the software to ensure knowledge retention by the organization or to meet regulatory requirements.

.1 Agile Techniques

- **Personas**: These may prove useful in assessing the needs and availability of the stakeholder groups for the necessary communication in an agile approach and how you will organize this agile communication.
- **Planning Workshop**: The planning workshop is generally used as the forum for establishing how the team will operate, including decisions about how the results of business analysis activities will be delivered and communicated to the team throughout the course of the project.

3.1.5   Plan Requirements Management Process (2.5)

In agile approaches, requirements management is focused on ensuring that the intake of new work by the team matches the priorities of the stakeholders and/or sponsor, and delivers value to the business. Agile approaches stress the importance of welcoming changing requirements. This means that the ordering of work items that are ready for development may be changed at any time.

.1 Agile Techniques

- **Backlog Management**: Most agile approaches use backlog management to determine which requirements are ready to be worked on by the development team.

3.1.6   Manage Business Analysis Performance (2.6)

This activity will be performed on an ongoing basis as the business analyst learns to work effectively with stakeholders and the development team. As everyone involved better understands how to work together to deliver value, the business analysis process, methods, or techniques in use may need to change. Effective business analysis performance will result in limited rework of the requirements documentation, effective prioritization and scoping of requirements, and clear communication of need to the development team.

.1   Agile Techniques

- **Retrospectives**: Retrospectives are a common practice used by agile teams seeking to improve their ways of working. Business analysts should look for feedback on the requirements they provide to the team and how and when those requirements are provided in order to find ways to improve their processes.
- **Value Stream Mapping**: Value stream mapping can be useful in assessing how business analysis activities are contributing to the delivery of value to the customer and identifying activities that may not be adding value.

3.2   Elicitation

Elicitation (Chapter 3 of the *BABOK® Guide*) describes how business analysts work with stakeholders to identify and understand their needs and concerns and understand the environment in which they work. Effective elicitation ensures that the stakeholders' actual underlying needs are understood, rather than stated or superficial desires. Elicitation is ongoing throughout the project and performed in conjunction with analysis activities (as compared to traditional approaches, where it is possible to perform elicitation as a distinct activity or phase).

On agile projects, the most common pattern is an initial elicitation activity which looks at the high level needs, goals, and scope of the solution. In every iteration, there is more detailed elicitation for the user stories which constitute the backlog items for that iteration.

3.2.1   Prepare for Elicitation (3.1)

Preparing for elicitation changes during the life of the project. Early on, it is done by the business analyst to coordinate supporting materials and schedule resources to define the high-level requirements. During this phase of the project, elicitation activities will generally be structured as more exploratory sessions to understand underlying needs, build out the initial list of feature requests, and determine what is most valuable to work on. As the project progresses, work is coordinated by prioritization of the backlog. This will often result in more structured and directed elicitation sessions designed to understand low-level details of a particular feature or requirement. Stakeholders may work directly with the developers to elaborate requirements. In that situation, the developer is performing business analysis activities for the project and should be trained in good business analysis practices. Where this is not possible, the business analyst will often act as a proxy. This task requires the scheduling of resources and the coordination of inputs to align with the progressive elaboration of the backlog.

In preparation for elicitation activities, it is recommended that the business analyst perform customer research and a stakeholder analysis to understand the needs, wants, and preferences of the stakeholders they will be working with. By tailoring elicitation discussions to the stakeholder, business analysts can maximize the efficiency and value of the elicitation session.

.1   Agile Techniques

- **Personas**: Personas may provide insight into the particular needs of a stakeholder or the techniques that will be most effective in understanding those needs.
- **User Story**: A user story will identify the role for whom the story provides value (and therefore identify the stakeholders who can elaborate on that value).
- **Story Mapping**: Developing a user story map with users and other stakeholders will ensure the stories implemented in the solution will come together as a cohesive product in the end.

3.2.2   Conduct Elicitation Activity (3.2)

Elicitation activities are conducted on a frequent basis throughout the project, possibly even daily. Early on, elicitation is performed to define high-level requirements or a vision for the product. As the project progresses, stakeholders interact with the development team directly during iteration planning and development. The intent of all elicitation activities is to generate just enough detail to ensure that the work at hand is performed correctly. These elicitation activities often occur in workshops with product users and other stakeholders who have a vested interest in the features or requirements being discussed.

.1   Agile Techniques

- **Behaviour Driven Development (BDD)**: Stakeholders may find it easier to articulate their needs by providing examples rather than through abstract models.
- **Collaborative Games**: Collaborative games encourage participants in an elicitation activity to collaborate in building a joint understanding of a problem or a solution.

Note: As mentioned above, analysis is usually performed during elicitation sessions. Most of the techniques found in the *Agile Extension,* as well as many of the techniques in the *BABOK® Guide,* are suitable for this purpose.

3.2.3   Document Elicitation Results (3.3)

A major value of documentation is that it can be used for long-term knowledge retention. Agile approaches aim to minimize the time between the development of requirements and their implementation in software, reducing the overall value of that documentation to the team. Records of elicitation activities should be kept to ensure that key decisions can be understood at a later date, or to ensure that regulatory or governance requirements are met. It is important to note that documentation should not be limited to purely textual artifacts to represent requirements and context for requirements. Visualizing requirements through models, mock-ups, and prototypes an be a quick mechanism for conveying a large amount of information about a solution. However, care should also be taken when using visualizations that mimic the solution, as it is important to define requirements without unnecessarily limiting the solution options.

.1 Agile Techniques

- **Lightweight Documentation**: See this section for guidelines on developing documentation. In most cases, there will not be separate documentation of the elicitation and analysis work.

3.2.4   Confirm Elicitation Results (3.4)

This will be performed by the team during iteration planning, throughout the development iteration, and at customer acceptance. The customer may change their mind about some specific element of a story after seeing the result. This feedback becomes an input into the conduct elicitation activity.

.1 Agile Techniques

- **Behaviour Driven Development (BDD)**: Elicitation outcomes will frequently be captured in the form of acceptance criteria that will be used by the team to verify that the software meets stakeholder needs. In behaviour or test driven development, examples are often used as the basis for generating acceptance criteria that can be used to confirm elicited requirements.
- **Retrospectives**: During retrospective sessions, the information that was elicited may be confirmed or refuted based on the perspective generated when a customer sees the product in action. This may result in modifications to the solution requirements.

3.3   Requirements Management and Communication

Requirements Management and Communication (Chapter 4 of the *BABOK® Guide)* describes how business analysts manage conflicts, issues, and changes in order to ensure that stakeholders and the project team remain in agreement on the solution scope, how requirements are communicated to stakeholders, and how knowledge gained by the business analyst is maintained for future use. This is not a one-time activity, but is performed continuously throughout the life of the project.

3.3.1   Manage Solution Scope and Requirements (4.1)

As agile projects unfold, the scope is defined with increasing specificity. Depending on the agile approach being used, the specific details of the scope can be found in the product backlog or a similar document. Content for the product backlog, user stories, or other requirements documentation managed in these activities is generated through elicitation activities, which are mentioned in the previous section. Based on the level of elaboration the product backlog itself may vary in its own level of detail. It should also be considered that the sponsor may decide to terminate the project should they decide that further efforts will not provide an acceptable return of business value.

.1   Agile Techniques

- **Backlog Management**: Most agile teams use the product backlog to manage both solution scope and requirements.
- **Story Decomposition**: Story Decomposition enables planning at the appropriate level of granularity and supports the just-in-time nature of agile approaches.

3.3.2   Manage Requirements Traceability (4.2)

On agile projects, everything is connected back to the strategic themes, epics, and stories that are used to define the project. This is maintained by the product owner or the business analyst.

.1   Agile Techniques

- **Story Decomposition**: When stories are decomposed into smaller, more granular pieces, retaining the larger epic or feature and tieing the decomposed story to its larger, parent concept can help create requirements traceability.
- **Story Mapping**: While story maps primarily show relationships between user stories, indicating a process or flow of activities, they also map user stories to larger activities that the user must be able to accomplish. As such, story mapping can serve as a tool to provide traceability between related stories and between stories and the larger activities they support.

3.3.3   Maintain Requirements for Reuse (4.3)

In mature agile organizations this happens much the same way as it does in traditional efforts, where documentation and prototypes are retained for the future development of the project or reused on similar, related efforts. The difference is in the way that requirements are documented throughout the life of the project or at the end of the project. In addition to product backlogs, user stories, and other standard requirements documentation, the source code itself is often written to be self-documenting. Information regarding the requirements the code satisfies can be included in the notes the developers create for the source code.

.1 Agile Techniques

- **User Story**: A well documented user story can be retained and re-used as a starting point for future refinements of the product or similar needs for another product.

3.3.4   Prepare Requirements Package (4.4)

Preparing the requirements package can be handled through techniques such as scenarios, use cases, acceptance tests, mock-ups, and models associated with the themes, epics, and stories used to define the project. This is an ongoing activity through the life of the development of the solution. The specific techniques used will depend upon the approach chosen at the beginning of the project, and will change based on the emergent understanding of what works best in the context of the project. Release planning often helps to guide how requirements should be packaged by understanding how the team is proposing to bundle features in planned product releases.

.1 Agile Techniques

- **Story Decomposition**: Epics, features, or minimally marketable features (MMF) tie groups of user stories together into larger packages that can be discussed with stakeholders.

3.3.5   Communicate Requirements (4.5)

In agile projects requirements are communicated to developers on an on-going basis. Requirements communication most often happens in release planning meetings where themes and stories are reviewed and selected for release. They are also discussed in more detail in iteration planning meetings where the models and specifications are selected and discussed among the team and the product owner. In these iteration planning meetings, risks are also reviewed and discussed. Additionally, daily team meetings are often used as an opportunity for developers to get clarification or identify ambiguous requirements, where the business analyst communicates the details of the requirements or clarifies ambiguity. Models and visualizations for requirements can be a quick way to communicate detailed requirements and facilitate understanding of the problem the solution needs to solve.

.1 Agile Techniques

- **Planning Workshop**: See this technique for further details.

3.4   Enterprise Analysis

Enterprise Analysis (Chapter 5 in the *BABOK® Guide)* describes how business analysts identify a business need, refine and clarify the definition of that need, and define a solution scope that can feasibly be implemented by the business. This knowledge area describes problem definition and analysis, business case development, feasibility studies, and the definition of solution scope. Enterprise analysis is about identifying the business need, opportunity or problem to be solved and deciding on the appropriate approach to addressing the need.

3.4.1   Define Business Need (5.1)

Define Business Need, as described in *BABOK® Guide*, extends to agile approaches.

.1 Agile Techniques

- **Business Capability Analysis**: A business need will usually correspond to the development of a new capability or the enhancement of an existing capability.
- **Collaborative Games**: Some collaborative games can be useful in exposing un-met business needs.

3.4.2 Assess Capability Gaps (5.2)

Assess Capability Gaps, as described in *BABOK® Guide,* extends to agile approaches.

.1 Agile Techniques

- **Business Capability Analysis**: This can be used to understand what shortcomings exist in an existing capability.

3.4.3 Determine Solution Approach (5.3)

Agile is a solution approach. It may be selected in order to provide a faster delivery of value than traditional approaches, or because the problem area needs to be explored. It also supports incremental delivery so the solution approach can be evolved over the course of the project. This approach provides flexibility in determining the best solution to a problem or opportunity being explored. A solution may begin as a custom developed evolutionary prototype, then transition to a customized COTS solution or become an integrated part of another product, for example. As such, on agile projects the solution approach can sometimes change during the course of development.

.1 Agile Techniques

- **Purpose Alignment Model**: The purpose alignment model can provide guidance regarding the best solution approach to take for a given business need.

3.4.4 Define Solution Scope (5.4)

The scope of agile projects evolves during the course of the project as the team learns more about ways to solve the problem and the customer preferences for a solution. The scope is defined in higher-level abstractions (such as themes and epics) and is detailed as the project evolves. These higher-level abstractions are important for scoping the solution and enabling the team to come up with an initial vision for the architecture and release plan for the product. This is often an iterative process, as scope may be refined based on what is technically feasible in an initial architecture assessment, impacting the release plan and project time lines. Similarly, the architecture plan may be modified or contain a phased approach to building out the infrastructure based on the planned high-level requirements that will be delivered in the release.

.1 Agile Techniques

- **Business Capability Analysis**: The scope of the project should be related to the business capabilities it is creating or enhancing.
- **Story Decomposition**: Epics and features can serve as the basis for defining the scope.
- **Story Mapping**: A story map can be used to see the relationship between the various stories delivered by the project.

3.4.5   Define Business Case (5.5)

The business case for agile projects is typically based on achieving a specific business outcome within a specified cost and time. The business case is revisited frequently as the team learns what it can deliver, how well it meets the real (not perceived) needs, and whether the business outcome and intended value can be achieved within the specified cost and time.

.1 Agile Techniques

- **Business Capability Analysis**: Defines the customer and organizational value associated with a business case.
- **Kano Analysis**: Identifies which product features are likely to have the greatest market impact.
- **Purpose Alignment Model**: Identifies what kind of investment is likely to generate the greatest value for the organization.
- **Real Options**: Allows assessment of when investment needs to be made in order to ensure value is obtained.

3.5   Requirements Analysis

Requirements Analysis (Chapter 6 in the *BABOK® Guide*) describes how business analysts prioritize and progressively elaborate stakeholder and solution requirements in order to enable the project team to implement a solution that will meet the needs of the sponsoring organization and stakeholders. It involves analyzing stakeholder needs to define solutions that meet those needs, assessing the current state of the business to identify and recommend improvements, and the verification and validation of the resulting requirements.

3.5.1   Prioritize Requirements (6.1)

On agile projects requirements are progressively elaborated. In other words, throughout the elicitation task elicitation results are progressively, or continually, broken down and elaborated. This is similar to the concept of continuous improvement, where the business analyst continually elaborates on the requirements to provide additional detail as needed and identifies new requirements that are prioritized based on the intended project outcomes. At each point of elaboration the constituent parts need to be evaluated and prioritized based on business value contribution and risk burn-down. In agile this is not a one-time up front activity. This happens throughout the life of the project on all remaining work and new work brought in from learning about the product.

.1   Agile Techniques

- **Backlog Management**: Backlog management is the standard method of prioritizing requirements in many agile approaches. The backlog can be re-prioritized whenever business needs change or are better understood.

- **Kano Analysis**: Kano analysis can provide insight into the relative importance of features to a user group.

- **Planning Workshop**: Prioritization normally takes place during a planning workshop.

Note: also see the expanded treatment of **MoSCoW Prioritization**.

3.5.2   Organize Requirements (6.2)

Due to the just-in-time, continual nature of requirements elicitation and documentation activities, it is important to think about how requirements will be organized for an agile project. For example, user stories can often show up in multiple documents that are dedicated to the user story that they describe. As a result it can make finding the appropriate requirements a cumbersome activity. While documentation on agile projects should be lightweight, it is still important to have a requirements management plan and method for organizing requirements that can be used by project team members and other stakeholders.

In agile, it can be valuable to organize requirements to minimize dependencies between feature sets. This reduces complexity and risk and improves testability at the business level value. Organizing requirements around business value and progressively elaborated requirements, as opposed to technical implementations, results in the solution being architected from a business standpoint. Exceptions do exist on projects such as component teams, where the business value arises from delivering enabling technology. Even then, these requirements need to be prioritized and filtered based on risk burn-down and business value contribution. Story maps within epics can be used as a method to organize requirements.

.1   Agile Techniques

- **Story Decomposition**: Individual stories may be organized around an epic or feature, where the epics and/or features are used as the organizational method.
- **Story Mapping**: Story mapping also shows how individual stories are related to or support one another. This may be used as a method for determining related stories and organizing those stories and their associated requirements based on those relationships.

3.5.3   Specify and Model Requirements (6.3)

At different levels of elaboration there are different methods for specifying and modeling requirements. The approach should support progressive elaboration, be adaptable to change based on learning, and not cause the team to select solutions too early. It should also ensure that intent and intended business value are communicated consistently through the elaboration. Agile teams tend to use stories and tasks at the lowest level of decomposition. These stories and tasks can be supported by detailed documentation and use cases. It is becoming increasingly common for acceptance tests to be produced as part of specifying and modelling the requirements.

.1 Agile Techniques

- **Behaviour Driven Development (BDD)**: Concrete examples of functionality may help stakeholders better specify and understand their needs, or deal with specific scenarios that are of greater value.
- **Storyboarding**: Used to describe user interface (UI) functionality and behaviour.

Note: also see the expanded treatment of **User Story** in this extension.

3.5.4   Define Assumptions and Constraints (6.4)

On agile projects defining assumptions and constraints is handled through a risk management approach. For example, some agile teams treat risks as stories within themes so that they can be tracked with the features or epics they pertain to. Risk mitigation activities would then be prioritized, burned down, and then re-prioritized as the stories are performed. This is typically produced by the individuals performing the business analyst and project manager functions, along with the support of the rest of the team. Prioritization would then be performed by the product owner or someone in an analogous role.

.1 Agile Techniques

- **Lightweight Documentation**: Assumptions and constraints can be documented in lightweight documentation that is created by the project team as it progresses with the project.
- **Personas**: Personas can be used as a way to track risks associated with a particular user group or stakeholder type that the product team should be aware of during development. Persona scan also be optionally modified to include information regarding any assumptions made about a stakeholder type during the stakeholder analysis.
- **User Story**: User stories can be modified to track assumptions or constraints (particularly the latter) related to a story. Team can also use the user story format as a way of collecting risks to be addressed by the team as an outstanding work item, although it

needs to be clear to the team and stakeholders that these are separate from the stories planned for development.

3.5.5 Verify Requirements (6.5)

Verification ensures that something has been designed to specification and adhering to quality standards. For example, verifying that a user story or other requirements document is properly structured, contains the appropriate fields, and contains the appropriate level of detail. Requirements are verified by the team throughout the course of the project. Through retrospectives and operations reviews, the team may decide to modify the level of detail of the requirements or the method of specifying and modeling requirements to improve the performance of the team. Verification of requirements usually is done through direct stakeholder interaction with the team as the software is developed, eliciting direct feedback from the team during retrospectives, daily team meetings, or other meetings or workshops.

.1 Agile Techniques

- **Retrospectives**: Retrospectives provide rapid feedback on what has been built to verify that what has been built will meet the desired business outcomes.
- **Story Mapping**: Story Mapping is a technique that enables confirming that the selected user stories will actually deliver the desired business outcomes.

3.5.6 Validate Requirements (6.6)

Validation ensures that a deliverable or product actually fulfills its intended purpose. For example, validating that a user story adequately describes the business process or activity that it is intended to describe. Requirements are validated throughout the development and delivery of the solution through continual involvement with the customer and, where applicable, the product owner or analogous role. This happens at many points during the project, such as release planning, iteration planning, during development, and at customer acceptance. Prototypes can also be an effective way to validate the utility of functionality relative to its intended purpose by giving a user something to test and try early in development with product review sessions to obtain feedback from the users on the evolution of the prototype.

.1 Agile Techniques

- **Behaviour Driven Development (BDD)**: In Behaviour or Test Driven Development, examples are used as a means for designed requirements and establishing acceptance criteria that can be used to design the solution. The ability to meet these real-world examples can serve as a means to validate solution requirements.

- **Retrospectives**: Retrospective sessions enable customers to assess the solution as it is being developed to validate whether or not it is on track to or successfully meets their needs.

3.6 Solution Assessment and Validation

Solution Assessment and Validation (Chapter 7 of the *BABOK® Guide*) describes how business analysts assess proposed solutions to determine which solution best fits the business need, identify gaps and shortcomings in solutions, and determine necessary work-a-rounds or changes to the solution. It also describes how business analysts assess deployed solutions to see how well they met the original need so that the sponsoring organization can assess the performance and effectiveness of the solution.

3.6.1 Assess Proposed Solution (7.1)

In agile projects solution assessment occurs continually as the solution is built and refined. Initial solutions options are identified up-front, with decisions that serve as a starting point for continual evolution of the product. Throughout the life of the product, as the business needs evolve or become more well defined, the team's understanding of the problem's solution will also evolve. With effective agile architecture and design, the cost of redoing components that have already been developed can be relatively low. With an agile cadence, assessing the proposed solution becomes an ongoing assessment of the solution options against the business case and current status of the project.

.1 Agile Techniques

- **Real Options**: Allows for assessment of aspects of the solution to determine when decisions have to be made regarding a particular proposal.

3.6.2   Allocate Requirements (7.2)

On agile projects, requirements allocation is done by allocating requirements into groups or categories. This can be done by looking for themes amongst proposed pieces of functionality that contribute to one or more features. Agile teams are typically small teams and this allocation shapes the design of the delivery organization itself. Feature teams form around the features and component teams supporting cross-feature requirements.

.1   Agile Techniques

- **Story Decomposition**: Breaks down high-level epics and features into smaller supporting stories which can be allocated to different components (including process or organizational changes).

3.6.3   Assess Organizational Readiness (7.3)

The organizational readiness assessment occurs on agile projects in much the same way as it does in traditional projects. The difference is that the release cadence can be more frequent. A significant area to define in agile projects is how often the organization can absorb releases. Organizational readiness should include not just the end-user/customer of the release, but the supporting organization as well (for example, support, training, sales, marketing, and accounting). An assessment should be made of what is required for a solution release to deliver value by considering things such as whether the product needs to be fully tested and what features are minimally required to achieve uptake and value for customers.

3.6.4   Define Transition Requirements (7.4)

The determination of transition requirements occurs in an agile project much as it does in a traditional project. The ability to deliver value incrementally opens up new possibilities for transition. Unlike a monolithic release, the organizational impact can be smaller but more frequent. Since the cost of development per unit is lower, temporary integration into existing systems can be developed, which makes the need for running parallel systems less significant. Transition requirements for agile should projects should be tracked, ensuring those requirements are met in the development, operations, and support plans for each delivery cycle of the product, as needed.

.1 Techniques

- **User Story**: User stories can be used for the planning of transition requirements, where they are prioritized and/or ordered in the same fashion as user stories for any other solution requirement. User stories can be accompanied with a list of acceptance tests that can be used to assess if the user story has been satisfied in the resulting product.

3.6.5 Validate Solution (7.5)

Validation of a solution happens as an ongoing effort in an agile project. Within each iteration, the customer is provided with detailed feedback on the current requirements. At the completion of each iteration cycle, the product owner facilitates alignment with the customer need and continued alignment with the business case.

.1 Agile Techniques

- **Retrospectives**: Retrospectives are reviews that examine if the piece of the product has been built in the current iteration meets the actual business need.

3.6.6 Evaluate Solution Performance (7.6)

Upon release, the product owner facilitates the understanding of how well the solution meets the needs of the customer. While the business analyst or product owner may also assess the utility and performance of the solution during any point in the delivery cycle, it is important to also pause at the end of the delivery cycle to assess the current state of the product in the context of the business value it needs to deliver to its users. The business analyst or product owner should ensure completed items meet expectations and identify new opportunities to add value for the business. As new items are uncovered a business analyst or product owner should assess the new requests against the product roadmap and business requirements to assess the relative value of the new item. The incremental nature of the backlog allows new higher-value items discovered during this evaluation to enter into the backlog ahead of existing items. This is likely to create changes to plans for subsequent delivery cycles; however, it also helps to ensure the features of the highest value are delivered first to shorten time to deliver value to the customer/user.

.1 Agile Techniques

- **Business Capability Analysis**: Allows business analysts and stakeholders to understand the importance and relative performance of a business capability.
- **Value Stream Mapping**: Used to identify those aspects of the solution that add value for customers and those which do not add value. This assessment becomes the basis for ongoing improvement efforts.

Agile Techniques

4.1   A Context for Agile Business Analysis

This chapter of the *Agile Extension to the BABOK® Guide* provides analysts with techniques and tools that will assist them in excelling in the agile world. In order for the techniques and skills presented in this section to be applied successfully, there are some foundational principles that need to be understood. These principles are supported by a number of practical techniques that can be used by practitioners when they undertake business analysis on agile projects.

The principles that guide successful business analysis can be categorized into two distinct frameworks:

- the Discovery Framework and
- the Delivery Framework.

The Discovery Framework deals with the whats and the whys of the product. Effective discovery is supported by three underlying principles:

- See The Whole,
- Think as a Customer, and
- Analyze to Determine What is Valuable.

The Delivery Framework deals with the hows and the whens of the product. Effective delivery is supported by four underlying principles:

- Get Real Using Examples,
- Understand What is Doable,
- Stimulate Collaboration and Continuous Improvement, and
- Avoid Waste.

Please note that these guiding principles are meant as a guide and not necessarily as hard and fast rules. For example, while Get Real Using

Examples is included in the Delivery Framework, the techniques described in this principle can certainly prove effective within the Discovery Framework as well.

The following table shows the *Agile Extension* techniques that support each principle.

TABLE 4.1 **Agile Extension Techniques**

Principles of Agile Business Analysis						
The Discovery Framework				**Delivery Framework**		
See the Whole	**Think as a Customer**	**Analyze to Determine What is Valuable**	**Get Real Using Examples**	**Understand What is Doable**	**Stimulate Collaboration and Continuous Improvement**	**Avoid Waste**
Business Capability Analysis	Story Decomposition	Backlog Management	Behaviour Driven Development	Relative Estimation	Collaborative Games	Lightweight Documentation
Personas	Story Elaboration	Business Value Definition		Planning Workshop	Retrospectives	
Value Stream Mapping	Story Mapping	Kano Analysis		Real Options		
	User Story	MoSCoW Prioritization				
	Storyboarding	Purpose Alignment Model				

d

4.2   A Note on Agile Extension Techniques

The techniques described here have proven value in supporting agile business analysis, but we do not claim that this list is all-inclusive or in any way canonical. The techniques here were selected based on the experiences of the team members, and represent both expansions to existing content in the *BABOK® Guide* and new techniques not described in the current version. Future versions of the *Agile Extension* will likely include new techniques, and it is also possible that some of the techniques listed here will be removed.

In addition, many of the techniques listed here may prove useful to business analysis practitioners who are not working on agile teams.

Agile approaches tend to focus on continuous improvement in their methods and technique. The techniques in the *Agile Extension to the BABOK® Guide* will be required to reviewed and updated on a regular basis.

4.3   BA Techniques Mapped to Agile Guidelines

The following table maps techniques as described in the *BABOK® Guide* to the principles for agile business analysis presented in this document.

TABLE 4.2 Business Analysis Techniques Mapped to Agile Business Analysis Guidelines

Business Analysis Technique	BABOK v.2 Chapter	See the Whole	Think as a Customer	Analyze to Determine What is Valuable	Get Real using Examples	Understand What is Doable	Stimulate Collaboration and Improvement	Avoid Waste
Acceptance & Evaluation criteria definition	9.1		✔		✔			✔
Base lining	4.1.5.2		✔	✔				✔
Benchmarking	9.2	✔						✔
Brainstorming	9.3						✔	
Business Rule Analysis	9.4	✔	✔		✔			✔

Business Analysis Technique	BABOK v.2 Chapter	See the Whole	Think as a Customer	Analyze to Determine What is Valuable	Get Real using Examples	Understand What is Doable	Stimulate Collaboration and Improvement	Avoid Waste
Checklists	6.5.5.2				✔			✔
Coverage Matrix	4.2.5.1	✔						✔
Data Dictionary and Glossary	9.5	✔			✔			✔
Data Flow Diagrams	9.6	✔			✔			✔
Data Modeling	9.7	✔			✔			✔
Decision Analysis	9.8				✔	✔		✔
Document Analysis	9.9	✔			✔			✔
Estimation	9.10			✔		✔		✔
Feasibility Analysis	5.3.5.2			✔		✔		✔
Focus Groups	9.11		✔	✔	✔			
Force Field Analysis	7.3.5.2	✔					✔	
Functional Decomposition	9.12		✔		✔	✔		✔
Interface Analysis	9.13		✔		✔	✔		✔
Interviews	9.14		✔				✔	
Lessons Learned Process	9.15	✔					✔	
Metrics and Key Performance Indicators	9.16	✔		✔			✔	✔
MoSCoW Analysis	6.1.5.2			✔		✔		
Non-functional Requirements Analysis	9.17		✔		✔			✔
Observation	9.18	✔			✔		✔	

d

Business Analysis Technique	BABOK v.2 Chapter	See the Whole	Think as a Customer	Analyze to Determine What is Valuable	Get Real using Examples	Understand What is Doable	Stimulate Collaboration and Improvement	Avoid Waste
Organization Modeling	9.19	✓		✓				✓
Problem or Vision Statement	5.4.5.2	✓	✓	✓				✓
Problem Tracking	9.20	✓	✓	✓	✓			✓
Process Modeling	9.21	✓			✓			✓
Prototyping	9.22		✓		✓	✓		✓
RACI Matrix	2.2.5.2	✓			✓			
Requirements Documentation	4.4.5.1							✓
Requirements for Vendor Selection	4.4.5.2							✓
Requirements Workshops	9.23	✓	✓		✓	✓		
Risk Analysis	9.24	✓		✓	✓	✓		✓
Root Cause Analysis	9.25	✓			✓		✓	✓
Scenarios and Use Cases	9.26	✓	✓		✓			
Scope Modeling	9.27	✓			✓	✓		✓
Sequence Diagrams	9.28	✓			✓			✓
Signoff	4.1.5.3							✓
Stakeholder Map	2.2.5.3	✓			✓			
State Diagrams	9.29	✓			✓			✓
Structured Walkthrough	9.30	✓	✓	✓	✓		✓	
Survey/ Questionnaire	9.31	✓		✓				✓
SWOT Analysis	9.32	✓		✓				
Timeboxing/ Budgeting	6.1.5.3			✓		✓		

Business Analysis Technique	BABOK v.2 Chapter	See the Whole	Think as a Customer	Analyze to Determine What is Valuable	Get Real using Examples	Understand What is Doable	Stimulate Collaboration and Improvement	Avoid Waste
User Stories	9.33	✔			✔			✔
Variance Analysis	2.6.5.2	✔					✔	✔
Vendor Assessment	9.34				✔			✔
Voting	6.1.5.4			✔		✔	✔	

d

4.4   Guidelines for Agile Business Analysis

The following 7 guidelines for practicing business analysis inside an agile context, are based on the values and principles of the Agile Manifesto. Together these guidelines embody the discipline of agile business analysis.

These guidelines provide valuable context when applying the various techniques described in this chapter:

- In an agile context, business analysis views the entire system of people, process, and technology to find where true value lies and to help organizations maximize the likelihood of delivering a valuable and valued solution.
- Agile analysis pays special attention to the voice of the customer to understand their values and expectations.
- To confirm what is valuable, it is common to use concrete examples to both elicit and validate product needs.
- Technology stakeholders are empowered by effectively analyzed needs. It helps them determine how much work they can deliver at any given point in time, identify product requirements options, and provide recommendations to business partners on solutions.
- Facilitative techniques enable efficient and effective collaboration and accelerate a team's ability to define and deliver products.
- Trust and safety are integral to healthy teams and allows them to transparently identify improvement opportunities. Improving both product and process is imperative; therefore agile teams continually strive to get better.
- Always be on the lookout for, and avoid, anything wasteful.

Adopting these guidelines requires leveraging, extending, and adapting foundational business analysis techniques. See "BA Techniques Mapped to Agile Guidelines" on page 49 for a matrix of business analysis techniques that may apply in an agile context.

4.5   The Discovery Framework

The Discovery Framework deals with the whats and the whys of the product. Effective discovery is supported by three underlying principles:

- See The Whole,
- Think as a Customer, and
- Analyze to Determine What is Valuable.

4.5.1   See The Whole

See the Whole is a concept that describes the need to look at a problem or opportunity in the context of the big picture, focusing on the business context and why a project is being undertaken. It describes not just what a system is but how it will be used. It is important to assess how the solution achieves something of value for its recipients. The value context for the solution is created by understanding both the solution and the stakeholders, and then articulating who they are and how they will find value in the solution. The ideas behind See the Whole are influenced by systems thinking.

On agile projects there is a high risk of getting mired in the details on each iteration. When developing the business case for a solution and performing iteration and release planning activities it is important to maintain the fidelity of the context. By doing so the context guides the next level of elaboration. By thinking about the strategic outcome for the solution, the delivery team moves from order takers to a group that delivers business value with less code bloat, scope creep, and never-ending project time-lines. Seeing the whole creates situation-appropriate context and a shared understanding of the business problem that needs to be solved, which in turn will guide decision making.

The following sections describe commonly used techniques for this principle:

- Business Capability Analysis,
- Personas, and
- Value Stream Mapping.

d

There are other techniques within the *Agile Extension to the BABOK® Guide*, the *BABOK® Guide*, and other ad hoc techniques that can be utilized here as well.

.1 Business Capability Analysis

Purpose

Provide a framework for product scoping and release planning by

- generating a shared understanding of the outcomes of a business or product,
- identifying alignment with a strategy and specific performance gaps, and
- providing a scope and prioritization filter that is stable and has low friction to maintain over time.

Description

Business capability analysis is the analysis of the performance and risk associated with a set of business capabilities to identify specific performance gaps and to prioritize these based on business value and risk. Business capabilities describe the ability of a business to act on or transform something that helps achieve a business goal or objective. Many product development efforts are an attempt to improve the performance of a business capability or to deliver a new business capability.

Agile approaches create a framework that facilitates frequent re-assessment of business needs and value. The direction of the business and the gaps required for the business to meet its objectives must be revisited for each iteration planning session, which generally occurs every 2-4 weeks in most agile life-cycles. This means that an agile project team must maintain a constant view of the business capabilities that are required for the business to be successful, particularly those that are in scope for the product being delivered.

Elements

Capabilities

Capabilities are the abilities in a business to perform or transform something. Capabilities should describe the purpose or outcome of the performance or transformation, not how the performance or transformation is performed. It describes the what, as opposed to the how. For example, sending a fax is not a capability; notifying the customer is the capability.

Using Capabilities

Capabilities impact business value through increasing or protecting revenue, reducing or preventing cost, improving service, achieving compliance, or positioning the company for the future in alignment with the business strategy. Not all capabilities have the same level of value. For example, while distributing payroll to employees is important to a company, it is likely neither of high business nor customer value. In other words, this may not be a capability that adds value for the company to build and maintain internally. There are various tools that can be used to make business and customer value explicit in a capability assessment.

Performance Expectations

Since capabilities identify the abilities required to perform or transform something, capabilities can be assessed to identify explicit performance expectations. When a capability is targeted for improvement, a specific performance gap can be identified. The performance gap is the difference between the current performance and the desired performance given the business strategy.

Risk Model

Risks in the performance of the capability fall into the following categories:

- business risk,
- technology risk,
- organizational risk, and
- market risk.

Strategic Planning

Business capabilities for the current state and future state of an organization can be used to determine where that organization needs to go in order to accomplish their business strategy and imperatives. As a result of performing a business capability assessment there is generally a set of recommendations or proposals for solutions that need to be put in place. This information forms the basis of a product road map and serves as a guide for release planning.

Capability Maps

Frequently organizations use capability maps to provide a graphic view of elements involved in business capability analysis. The

d

following illustration demonstrates one element of a capability map that would be part of a larger capabilities grid.

FIGURE 4.1 Sample Capability Map

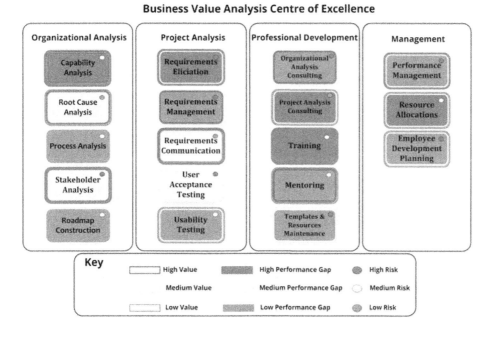

FIGURE 4.2 Sample Capability Map Cell

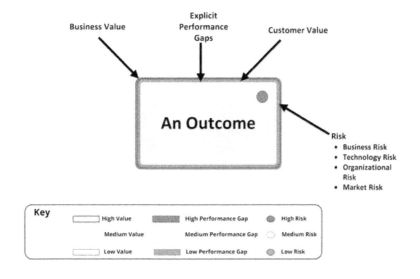

Usage Considerations

Capability analysis is useful when an organization changes its business focus or strategy, or there is more demand for change than there is capacity to deliver. When the demand outweighs the capacity to deliver, a large undifferentiated backlog of changes or improvement requests can result. Capability analysis helps to identify those improvement requests that will advance the strategic goals of the business. Upon completion of a project effort, the capability analysis can be updated to reflect improvements in performance and to identify the next most important capability performance gap to focus on.

The outcomes of a capability analysis serve as long-lived artifacts that represent a common view of the business. This can be used to generate shared understanding and align efforts. When the business strategy changes or customer desires evolve, this model can be used to rapidly re-prioritize the list of wants for a solution (for example, re-prioritizing the backlog).

Advantages

- The advantages of capability analysis are that they result in a shared articulation of outcomes, strategy, and performance. These help create very focused and aligned initiatives. The model works well with agile teams but it also helps identify opportunities that are not technology based, including process, talent, and data improvements.
- The capability analysis helps align business initiatives across multiple aspects of the organization.

Disadvantages

- This model requires an organization to agree to collaborate on this model.
- When this model is created unilaterally or in a vacuum it fails to deliver on the goals of alignment and shared understanding.
- The model also requires a broad, cross-functional collaboration in defining the capability model and the value framework.

.2 Personas

Purpose

User centered design practices often use personas as a powerful and simple tool to help design software that users will enjoy and benefit from.

Description

Personas are fictional characters or archetypes that exemplify the way that typical users interact with a product. They are often used in agile approaches to understand value from the perspective of a particular customer and allow a team that may not have direct access to a customer representative to better understand their needs. Work can then focus on the features of greatest value to a particular persona.

Elements

A persona should be described as though they are a real person. Personas may provide a name, personality, family, work background, skill level, preferences, behavior patterns, personal attitudes, goals, and needs. It is also a good practice to include a picture and write a short "day in the life" narrative that helps the team visualize the user.

Usage Considerations

Use personas when you want to get a deeper understanding of key stakeholders than one generally gets from a traditional role or actor description. Personas help drive products that are fit for purpose and highly usable, because they are patterned after the subtle qualities of real people that will interact with the systems and how they do their job.

If the data is available, using demographic (or anthropomorphic) data about the intended user population is a good way to start building personas. However in some cases it is necessary to be creative and invent personas based on little more than a few dry facts about the intended end users. In either case, a representative pool of personas should be identified.

Personas are then ranked to identify those will realize the most benefit from the system design.

Advantages

- Personas facilitate the shared understanding of specific requirements for different sets of users. These requirements can be visualized within the context of their user group and then used to develop user stories.

- Proposed solutions can be guided by how well they meet the needs of individual user personas. Features can be prioritized based on how well they address the needs of one or more personas.
- Provide a human "face" so as to focus empathy on the persons represented by the demographics.

Disadvantages

- Personas are fictional so there is often a tendency to create personas that embody traits that are common to most users, but in doing so creating a generic user that is not distinct or realistic. This can lead to software that is trying to be everything to everyone.
- Personas may not be a good substitute for a real user, if they are available. Personas can distance a team from a user community.

.3 Value Stream Mapping

Purpose

Value stream mapping (also known as material and information flow mapping) provides a complete, fact-based, time-series representation of the stream of activities required to deliver a product or service to the customer (internal or external). It is used to identify areas of potential improvement in an end-to-end process.

Description

A value stream represents the flow of material and information required to bring a product and/or service from raw material to the customer. A Value Stream Map (VSM) is a graphical representation that captures a snapshot of the value stream.

There are two main types of value stream maps that are widely used:

- **Current State Value Stream Map**: Depicts a value stream as it is applied by those who are responsible for executing it. It is usually used as a starting point for analysis of an existing process to identify improvement opportunities.
- **Future State Value Stream Map**: Derived from the current state and it shows what the value stream will look like after the implementation of the improvements.

In an agile environment, this diagram is usually simple and drawn on a whiteboard. It can be used to help re-engineer business processes to

d

optimize use of software. It can also be used to re-engineer and tune the software development process itself, for example, to reduce lead time from product discovery to release.

Elements

The following is a broad description for one approach to building a value stream map.

Prepare

1. Gather a cross-functional team. In the agile world this should include people with business domain knowledge and technical team members (such as developers, testers, and architects). Often someone acting as the business analyst will facilitate the session.

2. Assign a value stream map owner. Ideally this is someone who has a deep understanding of the current process.

3. Select a product, a product family, or a service, and define the scope of the value stream map.

4. Identify the customer value received so it can be traced back.

Create Current State

The current value stream map can be captured following these steps:

1. Observe or simulate value stream. Follow a product (or product family) path by starting at the end closest to the customer and record the process working your way backwards to the beginning.

2. Draw the value stream map.

3. Capture the information flow. The information that is vital for the value stream to function. Information flow includes (but not limited to) things such as orders, schedules, inventory time, changeover time, cycle time, and number of operators involved.

4. Build a model that shows each step in the flow with hand-offs and sequence. To assist in the analysis needed to identify opportunities for improvement in the process, ensure that you include time/cost values onto the steps in the process. These time values may be estimated, if needed. The more details available, the easier it is to identify improvement opportunities.

5. Validate the value stream map. The initial draft of the current value stream map must be validated before proceeding to the improvement phase.

Analyze Current State

The current value stream map can be analyzed as described in *Root Cause Analysis* of the *BABOK® Guide* version 2.0 (9.25 Root Cause Analysis) to identify value added steps (such as transformation processes) from those that are non-value added (such as excessive inventories).

The non-value added steps can be analyzed further to determine which ones are necessary (such as meeting regulatory requirements) and which ones are unnecessary (such as excessive paperwork).

Create Future State

The future state value stream map can be drawn as follows:

1. Identify improvement areas. Unnecessary non-value added steps are the source of waste and they can be eliminated. Team members can mark these areas (such as reducing lead time) on the current value stream map.

2. Capture the future state value stream map. Draw the value stream map that shows what the value stream will look like after you have eliminated the waste (unnecessary wait time, excessive administrative paperwork, high inventories, and so forth).

Once the future state is captured it can be used as the target state of the improvement initiative.

Implement Process Improvement

- Identify supporting material required for implementing the improvement such as information technology systems, training, and changeover.
- Implement the improvement.

In an agile project, value stream mapping will be most utilized when implementing process improvement. Often the changes to be made in the business process will require changes to or implementation of supporting software products. The requirements for these changes or enhancements become backlog items that feed into an agile initiative.

Once the improvement is made, the future state becomes the current value stream map and it can be used as a starting point for another improvement cycle.

d

The following is an example of a value stream map.

FIGURE 4.3 **Value Stream Map**

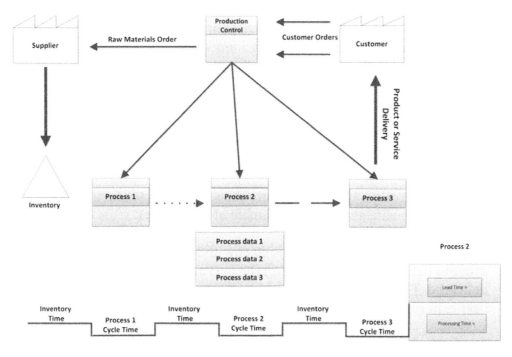

Usage Considerations

Advantages

- More comprehensive than a process flow diagram.
- Provides a blueprint for implementing improvement.
- Establishes a shared understanding of process wastes and bottlenecks.
- Provides a common visual language for diverse stakeholders.

Disadvantages

- Not easy to construct in comparison with other visual modeling techniques.
- Can look daunting because of all the information captured.
- Mapping paralysis. It is easy to get caught making the current state value stream map complete and perfect instead of proceeding to the improvement stage.
- Doesn't work well in knowledge based or non-linear work.
- Leads to disruptive or "re-engineering" approach. Doesn't work well with ongoing improvement efforts.

4.5.2   Think as a Customer

Thinking like a customer is a key component of agile business analysis. The customer is the person who gets value from the product we are building. We start with a high level view of customer goals and progressively decompose these into a more and more detailed understanding of the specific needs that the product must meet.

Agile processes incorporate feedback loops to continuously validate this understanding. As product delivery progresses, the customer and team understanding of the needs will evolve, it is important that these changes influence and define the work of the team going forward.

Agile analysis slices the delivery into the smallest practical increments that deliver business value over the life of the project.

It is important that agile analysis start with a holistic perspective, in order to help the team understand the overall product that needs to be delivered. The team collaborates with the customer to consider the user experience expected.

A goal of analysis is to ensure the voice of the customer, especially the end-user, is elicited and expressed in the product.

Backlog items represent work to be done and convey customer thinking, and can be represented through prototypes, user stories, use cases, minimal marketable features, features, epics, or work items.

The following sections describe commonly used techniques for this principle.

The techniques listed below are based on user stories:

- Story Decomposition,
- Story Elaboration,
- Story Mapping, and
- User Story.

A technique for prototyping a user interface and using that to define detailed requirements is:

- Storyboarding.

d

There are other techniques within the *Agile Extension to the BABOK® Guide*, the *BABOK® Guide*, and other ad hoc techniques that can be utilized here as well.

.1 Story Decomposition

Purpose

Story decomposition is a derivation of existing requirements analysis techniques such as functional decomposition. In an agile context, stories are often used to represent the work of the team and the requirements (or acceptance criteria) of that work. Story decomposition ensures that the requirements for a product are represented at the appropriate level of detail and are derived from a valuable business objective.

This technique provides a structure for defining the various elements of requirements at progressively smaller levels of granularity, starting with the broad system context and drilling down in multiple levels to eventually define the detailed acceptance criteria for individual user stories.

Description

The most common agile approach to story decomposition can be described as "breadth-before-depth":

- start with a very high level picture of what business goals need to be achieved,
- decompose those into smaller components that provide increments of valuable functionality (sometimes called minimally marketable feature sets or MMFs. Minimal viable products or MVPs are the aggregation of multiple MMFs), and
- split the components into user stories, and eventually elaborate the user stories with acceptance criteria, see "Story Elaboration" on page 68.

A story that is too large or insufficiently understood to elaborate, estimate, or deliver as a story is sometimes called an epic. Epics, when used, are later decomposed into smaller stories.

FIGURE 4.4 **Story Decomposition**

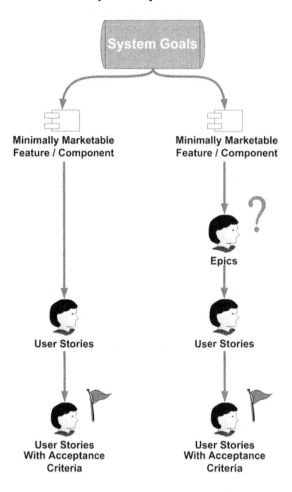

Different teams apply this technique in different ways. For example, some teams follow the model linearly, as shown in the above diagram, while other teams utilize techniques that work best in their environment. For example, once a team has developed the MMF (sometimes referred to as feature groups), they may employ use cases instead of stories. The analyst's role here is to focus on dynamic collaboration, facilitation, and communication in getting acceptance for just what is required to develop and deliver the product.

d

The following table describes the different levels of story decomposition.

TABLE 4.3 Story Decomposition

Level	Description
System Goals	The product goals are the highest level of business requirements. They represent the business drivers for undertaking the project and form the rationale against which all of the detailed level needs are assessed.
MMF/ Component	MMF stands for Minimal Marketable Feature. Minimal Viable Products or MVPs are the aggregation of multiple MMFs. These are logical groupings of functionality and capabilities the delivered product needs to provide to be worth releasing. Often these will form the themes for a single release and serve to provide a big-picture context for the product being developed.
Epic	A piece of functionality that enables a user to achieve a clearly identified business objective. Often epics are at the level of elementary business processes---a piece of work undertaken by one person, at one time, in one place that delivers on a specific operational objective. Epics are often a user story that is too large to fit into an iteration. Therefore it requires story decomposition in order to break it into less than iteration sized stories.
User Story	Represents a user requirement that is to be implemented in the delivered system. The user story is the most common backlog item used in agile projects.
Acceptance Criteria	Conditions of satisfaction or criteria needed to validate a user story. Can be written as lists of items, specifications, or user acceptance tests (or a combination). Detailed requirements are represented and validated in the acceptance criteria.

Usage Considerations

Story Decomposition is undertaken progressively. One of the most significant differences between agile projects and plan-driven projects is in the definition of detailed requirements. In agile projects the initial analysis activities will identify the goals, MMFs, and most of the epics. The initial set of user stories (probably for the first release of the product) will be done in the project initiation activities. There is a clear understanding that these stories are likely to change and that the teams' understanding of the requirements will evolve over time. Therefore, decomposing to the lowest level of detail is likely to be a wasteful activity early in the project.

Advantages

- This decomposition technique helps avoid the common problem of getting lost in the detail of the user stories and losing the big-picture context.

- It is important that team members keep the project's goals and objectives in mind, and while using the decomposition approach they are able to trace implemented or requested functionality back to the driving business objectives.

- Breaking the product into MMFs and epics helps with release-level planning, provides visibility into the development project, and helps coordinate external program activities such as organizational change management and user training.

Disadvantages

- A common anti-pattern is the temptation to treat story decomposition as a way of reverting to detailed requirements up-front. Ensuring the continued emphasis on just-enough and just-in-time, means knowing when to stop decomposing.

.2 Story Elaboration

Purpose

Story elaboration is a technique used to define the detailed design and acceptance criteria for a user story on a just-in-time/just-enough basis. Story elaboration is an ongoing activity that is part of the development process.

Description

Story elaboration is the lowest level of story decomposition and the process by which the story sentence is into broken down into pieces of work. This is often done by someone on the team who has strong business analysis skills, particularly with facilitation and communication. Story elaboration is the technique through which detailed requirements are elicited and communicated to the project team.

During each iteration, the team that works on a story schedules time to expand on the story to understand the detail. Often (but not always) this is completed in a short workshop with the programmers who will work on the story, the business SME or customer who needs the story, the person who will test the story, and someone acting as a business analyst to facilitate and challenge the story. Typically, story elaboration is undertaken a few days ahead of the development of the story.

Story elaboration should be done on an as-needed, just-in-time basis for stories that have been determined to be in scope for the upcoming iteration. The project team should not investigate stories for further

d

elaboration if they have not been planned for the release in question, as the information collected may be stale and out of date.

Story elaboration is a communication technique that helps ensure the correct product is built. In an agile project, the detailed requirements are produced by story elaboration. However, as opposed to plan-driven approaches, and consistent with the just-in-time philosophy of agile, the detailed requirements defined during story elaboration contain only the requirement details for the piece of work that is to be completed in the coming release.

Elements

The result of story elaboration is a shared understanding among the participants of what the story means and what should be delivered to achieve the "Done" state for this story. The role of the business analyst in developing and communicating dynamic requirements necessitates a high degree of skill in both facilitation and communication.

Some teams uses tasks as a way to communicate their analysis of the user story. The outputs of effective story elaboration describe and/or document tasks that enable the team to successful deliver the upcoming iteration. These outputs may include

- task definitions and breakdowns,
- examples and scenarios that explain the customer's intent for the story,
- low-fidelity models that clarify the technical or process design (for example, data models, and data flow diagrams),
- screen or report mock-ups,
- acceptance criteria (test design specifications) to clarify how the story will be tested, often in the <given><when><then> format of behavior driven development,
- input/output data tables, and
- other artifacts that will be useful in the development and testing of this story.

Usage Considerations

Advantages

- The major advantage of story elaboration is that it decreases elicitation time, and potentially documentation, by focusing on current features. By elaborating on requirements only as they are needed, the team avoids the work of eliciting requirements for features that may never be built or that will need to be changed by the time they are ready for implementation.

Disadvantages

- For those who are relatively new to agile approaches, it can be difficult to determine the best timing for conducting a story elaboration. If conducted too early, the information may no longer be correct for the given release and will need to be re-elicited. However, when collected too late, it can delay project team progression to development.
- Another challenge to implementing story elaboration is the ability to elicit the appropriate level of detail such that the requirements can be developed, tested, and compared to acceptance criteria.

.3 Story Mapping

Purpose

Story mapping provides a visual and physical view of the sequence of activities to be supported by a solution. It uses a two-dimensional grid structure to show sequence and groupings of key aspects of the product on the horizontal dimension, with detail and priority of stories on the vertical dimension.

Description

A story map is a tool to assist in creating understanding of product functionality, the flow of usage, and to assist with prioritizing product delivery (such as release planning). It is also decomposition technique that allows for the evolutionary understanding of a product starting with an end-to-end view and drilling down to the detailed user stories.

A story map is designed to be an information radiator, used to visualize a product's requests in the context of usage and priority. The story map is often placed on display for the project team during release planning sessions. By analyzing the story map, the team can more readily identify dependencies generated as a result of the intended flow through the user stories. The map can also be used for risk assessment and management by examining how the stories will need to work together in the context of delivering business value.

d

The following illustration is an example of a story map.

FIGURE 4.5   Story Map

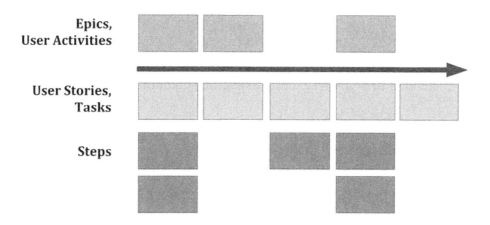

Elements

The story map has a central backbone of elements that will make up the product. Above this backbone are the large feature sets (activities) that need to be delivered over the life of the project. The backbone is a sequential set of tasks that need to be enabled by the software. Below the backbone are the detailed stories that implement the specific pieces of functionality to enable the tasks to be accomplished.

Usage Considerations

Advantages

- When the larger context of a product is not accounted for, agile projects can be subject to getting mired in the details with an inability to effectively string components together to create end-to-end business value. Story mapping helps avoid the common problem of getting lost in the detail of the user stories and the risk of losing the big-picture context.

Disadvantages

- Story mapping can become cumbersome where the product is very large and may require building a number of story maps that cover a large program of work. While story maps illustrate a flow, they do not analyze or illustrate dependencies between requirements (though they can be used to help facilitate that analysis).

- Environments that are not process oriented will find story maps less useful.

.4 User Story

User Stories are described in detail in the *BABOK® Guide* version 2.0 (9.33 User Stories). This information found here reflects and expands on that information in the context of agile development approaches.

Purpose

A user story represents a small, concise statement of functionality needed to deliver value to a specific stakeholder.

User stories can be used

- to capture and prioritize user needs,
- as a basis of estimating and planning product delivery,
- as a basis for generating user acceptance tests,
- as a way to monitor progress in delivering of value,
- as a unit for tracing related requirements,
- as a basis for additional analysis, and
- as a unit of project management and reporting.

Description

User stories are a planning technique that enables agile teams to track features of value to a customer or end user, and are used as a basis for estimating work. Typically, they are one or more sentences written by the customers, product owners, or business analysts that describe something of value to a stakeholder. User stories provide a mechanism for the product owner to scope, coordinate, and prioritize the increments of user value for development. A story should be short enough to be written on a small paper note card, usually a 3×5 inch index card or sticky note. Stories may also be recorded in an electronic system.

User stories capture stakeholder needs using short, simple documentation and invite exploration of the requirements through conversations, tests, and supplemental requirements representations as needed. They are concise and easy to change as stakeholder needs are better understood or as those needs evolve.

Some teams make use of other types of stories to catalogue, estimate, plan, and track other work needed to build the product. These stories typically define work needed to enable product development, deployment, and support.

d

A commonly used construct for ensuring quality in user stories is the INVEST criteria, which call for user stories to be

- Independent,
- Negotiable,
- Valuable,
- Estimable,
- Small, and
- Testable.

Elements

Title (optional)

The title of the story describes an activity that the user wants to carry out with the system. Typically, it is an active-verb goal phrase, similar to the way use cases are titled.

Description

There is no mandatory structure for user stories; however, the most popular format includes three components:

- a user role or persona [WHO],
- a necessary action, behaviour, or feature [WHAT], and
- the benefit or business value received by the user when the story is implemented [WHY].

Usage example:

"As a < role>, I need to < behavior > so that < business value >."

An alternative format is: "In order to < business value >, as a < role >, I need to < behavior >."

This canonical format can also be used for stories used to identify quality attributes. For example:

"As a Security Officer, I need to only allow authorized users to access the xyz functionality so I can ensure we enforce abc security directive".

Conversation

User stories serve as a reminder that the team needs to explore and understand the feature described in the story and the value that it will deliver to the customer. The story itself doesn't capture everything there is to know about the customer need, and the information implied by the story can be supplemented by analysis models to promote shared understanding.

Acceptance Criteria

When a user story is well defined and understood, it is accompanied by acceptance criteria. Acceptance criteria define the boundaries of a user story and help product owners, customers, or business analysts to answer what they need to provide value with the product.

Acceptance criteria help developers identify when to stop adding more functionality and to derive tests for verification and validation purposes. They can also be developed as a story becomes well understood to enable the development team to verify that the solution will meet the user's needs.

Usage Considerations

Advantages

- Tied to small, implementable, and testable slices of functionality facilitating rapid delivery and frequent customer feedback.
- Easily understandable by stakeholders.
- Can be developed through a variety of elicitation techniques, including but not limited to facilitated workshops, contextual inquiry, and other ethnographic elicitation techniques.
- User stories are simple enough that people can learn to write them in a few minutes, being careful about always delivering business value.
- The process of collaborating on defining and exploring stories builds team commitment and shared understanding of the business domain.
- Stories invite conversation for further decomposition and exploration.
- To facilitate estimating, planning, and delivery, many agile teams supplement stories with analysis models (such as a data model, business rules, user acceptance tests, screen mock-ups or prototypes, context diagram, and state diagram).

Disadvantages

- This conversational approach can challenge the team, since they do not have all the answers and detailed specifications up front.
- Too many stories can inflate the backlog.
- Large, chunky stories (epics) can be vague and difficult to use without breaking them down into small stories.

d

- Stories spawn more stories via decomposition so the information must be organized to ensure it is current and relevant (called pruning or grooming).
- The collection of stories needs to be managed (for example, with backlog management).
- Stories require context. If the team doesn't trace stories back (through validation) or supplement them with higher-level analysis and vision artifacts, then the team can lose sight of the big picture.
- Some practitioners can be confused about the difference between use cases, user stories, and story techniques.

.5 Storyboarding

Purpose

Storyboarding is used in conjunction with other techniques such as use cases, user stories, and prototyping to detail visually and textually the sequence of activities summing up different user interactions with the system or business.

Storyboarding serves

- to elicit, elaborate, organize, and validate the requirements,
- to communicate to developers what needs to be built,
- to assisting in user interface design,
- to show different variations of the proposed solution,
- to align stakeholders with the vision of the proposed solution, and
- as an input to tests.

Description

Storyboards (also known as dialogue map, dialog hierarchy, or navigation flow) use representative images and text to describe a task, a scenario, or a story. It can also be used with prototyping to represent parts of the system that are well understood or expensive and unnecessary to produce via formal prototypes.

When used to describe the interaction with the system, the storyboard shows how screens will look and how they will flow from one to another. When used to describe business organization, the storyboard shows the interaction with a business process such as back office.

Storyboards can be developed using white-boards and sticky notes or using software.

Storyboards are common in many analysis and development approaches, and are a form of prototyping (see the *BABOK® Guide* version 2.0 9.22 Prototyping). However, as agile approaches favour the development of working, usable software over throwaway prototypes, storyboarding is a useful tool for understanding how people will actually use the system.

Elements

Storyboards can be created in a workshop environment with relevant stakeholders.

Preparation

1. Identify main scenarios within the scope of the project. This can be derived from use cases or user stories or can be identified in a customer visit or an information-gathering session with experts.

2. Select the scenarios that need to have a storyboard developed. While some scenarios need to be detailed in a storyboard, others are obvious and can be omitted such as alternate scenarios and exceptions.

3. Identify participants and schedule the session.

4. Arrange room and equipment such as flip charts, markers, glue, scissors, rulers, printers, and access to the internet.

Session

1. Have attendees create illustrations for the storyboards of the selected scenarios.

2. Enhance storyboard illustrations with textual information such as optional interactions, unavailable interactions, further stakeholder requests not associated with the primary scenario, and general notes associated with a specific step.

3. Make sure each storyboard stands on its own by adding required explanations as text.

Wrap up

At the end of the session, the business analyst reaches consensus on the high level flow of the developed storyboards.

After the workshop, the company templates may be used to formally document the outcome of the session, adding additional elements to the storyboards such as storyboard identification, description, user, trigger, input, output, and issues.

d

Usage Considerations

Advantages

- Storyboarding can significantly reduce abstractness caused by other techniques such as use cases and user stories.
- Storyboards can be produced quickly and at a very low cost compared to other techniques such as prototypes.
- The intuitive nature of the storyboard encourages stakeholder participation.

Disadvantages

- Different look and feel than the final product.
- Easy to get bogged down on how, rather than why.

4.5.3   Analyze to Determine What is Valuable

The agile approach continuously assesses and prioritizes business value to ensure that the most valuable work is delivered at any point in time, always using the end customer perspective. It is also imperative to question the purpose behind requirements, challenging those requirements that do not support the business goals. Agile approaches enable the art of maximizing the amount of work not done, something essential to deliver valuable software early and continuously. The techniques outlined in this section facilitate the valuation of product needs on an on-going basis.

The following sections describe commonly used techniques for this principle:

- Backlog Management,
- Business Value Definition,
- Kano Analysis,
- MoSCoW Prioritization, and
- Purpose Alignment Model.

There are other techniques within the *Agile Extension to the BABOK® Guide*, the *BABOK® Guide,* and other ad hoc techniques that can be utilized here as well.

.1 Backlog Management

Purpose

The backlog is a wish list of requests for features to be included in a product, and is the main mechanism for managing requirements on an agile project.

Description

The product backlog is established at the beginning of a project. The backlog is a fluid collection of stories that evolves over the course of the project as more is learned about the product and its customers. The product owner is responsible for ordering the items on the backlog based on business value, feature importance, or other relevant criteria. When managing a backlog, items should be ordered such that the most important items occur at the top of the list and are ordered based on descending priority.

During the planning sessions, items are selected from the backlog based on factors such as priority, risk, value to the product or customer, and ability to deliver the feature within the given release. At the end of each release, feedback on what was developed may result in new items being added to the backlog, changed priorities, or removed items.

The backlog is developed at the beginning of an agile project, but it does not need to be complete at this time since it will continue to evolve throughout the project.

The backlog is sometimes referred to as a portfolio of options that the business can invest in. Other terms used are master story list and prioritized feature list.

Elements

Items in the Backlog

The backlog can contain user stories, use cases, features, functional requirements, and quality attribute stories as well as items that have been added by the team to support development of the requirements such as technical infrastructure. To aid in ordering the backlog, items should be expressed in such a way that the business value of the items is clear. Product risk mitigation items may also get added to the backlog as stories or pieces of work to be done.

Appropriate level of detail

Items with high order in the backlog will be developed in near-term releases, so they need to be detailed enough to allow the development team to estimate them with accuracy and be able to decompose them into the tasks needed to develop them, if needed. Items with lower priority can remain high-level and less precise until they rise in the order and need to be specified in more detail. Large items in the backlog are sometimes referred to as epics or MMFs, and may be broken down into multiple, more granular items as the backlog is elaborated via story decomposition. Some aspects of the story may be important near-term and others less important.

Estimation Accuracy

Items with high order in the backlog need to be estimated with enough accuracy to use them for planning releases. Items in lower order also need to be estimated, but with less accuracy since they are often less detailed. Estimates for time to complete items is often maintained within the backlog itself.

Prioritization

Items in the backlog are ordered relative to each other. Ordering can be established using numbering, value points, high/medium/low, or any other prioritization technique. The order of items on the backlog is likely to change over the course of the project, especially as the product evolves and the team receives feedback from the stakeholders and customers. It is important to note that ordering near term items is valuable, but putting a lot of effort into ordering the backlog far into the future can be a wasteful activity because the farther out backlog items are subject to change.

Managing Changes to the Backlog

The backlog is the main mechanism for both managing change to the requirements on an agile project and for controlling scope. When new or changed requirements are identified, they are added to the backlog and ordered relative to the other items. The backlog is also used to track and manage reported defects or bugs. Ordering the entire backlog can be done up front using relative importance designations (based on business value), which allows high-level prioritization without getting into too much detail. Since releases and iterations are time-boxed on agile projects, the items lower on the backlog are often not included in a given release. Rigorous ordering of the backlog allows the team to control the scope of the project and releases.

When an item is developed and accepted by the product owner, the item is removed from the backlog. The product owner role is responsible for managing the backlog, adding and ordering new or changed items, removing completed items, and revising the order on an ongoing basis. This process is sometimes referred to as pruning or grooming the backlog.

Usage Considerations

Advantages

- Since the requirements on the backlog are ordered in importance, the team knows that what they are working on in a given iteration is high priority and will contribute business value to the product. The members of the team responsible for detailing the requirements can review the backlog and determine if the items that will be developed in an upcoming release require further analysis in order to ready them for development.
- Since each release typically implements a small set of requirements, requirements are analyzed in detail on a just-in-time basis. What the team and the stakeholders learn about the requirements developed during a release can inform the analysis of other requirements in upcoming iterations.

Disadvantages

- Large backlogs may become cumbersome and difficult to manage. Breaking the overall product backlog into backlogs for releases (called release backlogs) can help address this disadvantage. Also, a lack of detail in the stories in the backlog can result in lost information over time.

.2 Business Value Definition

In order for a project to deliver value, the project team must first be able to identify whether a request is actually valuable to the organization. Without a clear understanding of business value, it is possible for the project to deliver something that sounds valuable but is actually not.

A project creates business value when it delivers anything that contributes to an organization's stated primary goals, for example

- increasing or protecting revenue,
- reducing or avoiding costs,
- improving service,

d

- meeting regulatory or social obligations,
- implementing a marketing strategy, and
- developing staff.

Often projects create options for the business to exploit. For example, the option to sell 1000 items of a product a day.

Business value should be expressed as a range or set of benefits. The evolution of clarity about business value will develop understanding of why the project is needed. The most important aspect of expressing business value is the conversation that generates the shared understanding.

Examples of bad business value statements are:

- This enables straight through processing.
- This will make 1 million dollars.
- This will save 1 million dollars.
- Mr. Big needs this product.

None of these show alignment with the goals of the organization.

Examples of good business value statement are:

- This project will generate an additional $20 million in profit. The model is based on the following assumptions:* We maintain 25% of the sales of existing product XYZ ($150 million a year).
- The total cost of designing, producing, and marketing the product is $7.5 million.
- Our product is first to market.
- We are able to release the product in the spring.

This statement conveys understanding of why the project is needed and would likely promote valuable conversation that generates a shared understanding of the project.

.3 Kano Analysis

Purpose

Kano analysis helps an agile team understand which product characteristics or qualities will prove to be a significant differentiator in the marketplace and help to drive customer satisfaction.

Description

Kano analysis assists in identifying features that will have the greatest impact on customer satisfaction, either because they are exceptionally important or because their absence will cause intense dissatisfaction. This helps the team determine which features are most important to implement before releasing a product to market.

Kano analysis rates product characteristics on two axes:

- the extent to which the feature is implemented in the product, and
- the level of customer satisfaction that will result from any given implementation level.

The resulting graph is plotted on a 2×2 matrix. Based on the resulting profile, the product characteristic should fall into one of three categories:

- threshold characteristics,
- performance characteristics, and
- excitement characteristics.

This analysis can then be used to try and identify characteristics that will give the product a unique position in the marketplace.

Elements

Threshold Characteristics

Threshold characteristics are those that are absolutely necessary for stakeholders to consider adopting a product. Their absence will cause intense dissatisfaction but, as they represent minimum acceptance criteria, their presence will not increase customer satisfaction beyond a certain low level. The challenge with eliciting requirements for these features is that people expect them to be present and so tend not to think about them unless explicitly asked.

Performance Characteristics

Performance characteristics are those for which increases in the delivery of the characteristic produce a fairly linear increase in satisfaction. They represent the features that customers expect to see in a product (speed, ease of use, etc). Requirements for these types of features are likely to most readily come to mind for the majority of stakeholders.

d

Excitement Characteristics

Excitement characteristics are those that significantly exceed customer expectations or represent things that the customer did not recognize were possible. Their presence will dramatically increase customer satisfaction over time. As these characteristics are not met by anything currently on the market, stakeholders will not tend to think about requirements that describe them.

Usage Considerations

In order to determine the category to which a characteristic or feature belongs, customers can be surveyed using two forms of a question about the feature:

- Functional form: How do you feel if this feature or characteristic is present in the product?
- Dysfunctional form: How do you feel if this feature or characteristic is absent in the product?

Possible answers to each question form are:

- I like it that way.
- I expect it to be that way.
- I am neutral.
- I can live with it that way.
- I dislike it that way.

Determining the category is based on mapping the answers to both forms of the question to the following grid. The top row represents the answers to the dysfunctional form of the question. The left column represents the answers to the functional form of the question.

TABLE 4.4 Kano Analysis Questions Grid

	Like	Expect	Neutral	Live With	Dislike
Like	Q	E	E	E	P
Expect	R	I	I	I	T
Neutral	R	I	I	I	T
Live With	R	I	I	I	T
Dislike	R	R	R	R	Q

E = Exciters

P = Performance

T = Threshold

I = Indifferent (Does not fit into one of the 3 categories)

Q or **R** = Questionable or Reversed (the answer doesn't make sense)

This approach is most applicable for consumer products or goods that will be resold, as it focuses on identifying requirements that will encourage widespread use or adoption of a product. The categorization of a particular characteristic tends to shift over time, as customers grow to expect features or characteristics to be present in a product. Exciters eventually become a standard expectation and threshold characteristic (think of the novelty of ATMs when they were first introduced; now customers assume their bank will have ATMs).

.4 MoSCoW Prioritization

Purpose

To identify the most critical set of features or stories that will deliver business value and produced a sequenced, prioritized list.

Description

MoSCoW is a method to prioritize stories (or other elements) in incremental and iterative approaches. MoSCoW provides a way to reach a common understanding on relative importance of delivering a story or other piece of business value in the product.

All stories in the backlog are valuable, but often not all of them can be delivered at the same time. MoSCoW provides a mechanism for

d

prioritizing stories in a backlog across multiple releases. Prioritization is important for any software development approach, but agile approaches cannot succeed without constant and frequent prioritization of work.

MoSCoW gets its name from an acronym formed by the following classifications of priority: Must have, Should have, Could have, and Won't have. The letter o is added to make the acronym pronounceable. The classifications are as follows:

- **Must**: The user stories that add significant value and constituent the Minimal Marketable Feature set.
- **Should**: The user stories that add distinct value, but are not required features.
- **Could**: The user stories that add some value, but have minimal impact on features.
- **Won't**: The user stories that add little to no value, and will not be included as features.

There is an expectation that priorities can change over the life of a project, and priorities are reassessed on a regular basis.

Elements

Product Backlog

A collection of user stories describing the desired functionality of a product.

Strategy

An understanding of the outcomes for an initiative.

Customer Preference

Clarity on what is most important to the customer.

Usage Considerations

MoSCoW is useful when trying to prioritize a backlog. Unlike some prioritization methods, this model helps differentiate between a set of useful user stories from those specifically focused on an outcome. After grouping the backlog elements in the MoSCoW categories it is important to then sequence at least the Must Have and Should Have elements into a ranked/numbered order as this will be used to sequence the work on the backlog items.

Some tools may not support MoSCoW as a prioritization structure and may need to be configured to support it, in which case an alternate categorization may be appropriate such as "High, Medium, Low".

Advantages

- MoSCoW is easy to describe and typically is powerful in prioritizing backlogs.

Disadvantages

- MoSCoW can be subjective. If there is not effective collaboration among the team members with a careful focus on business value this method of prioritization can be inaccurate.
- On a project where a business value increments approach (Minimal Marketable Features) is used, the team should only deliver Must Haves in the increment. MoSCoW is therefore inappropriate, however it is still important to provide a sequenced list to provide guidance for the order in which work should be undertaken.

.5 Purpose Alignment Model

Purpose

The purpose alignment model is used to assess ideas in the context of customer and business value. From an agile perspective, the model aids in making prioritization decisions and focusing investment on those features or capabilities that are of greatest value to the organization.

Description

The purpose alignment model is used to rate activities, processes, products, or capabilities in two dimensions, and use that information to help recommend the best actions to take to improve them based on those ratings. The first dimension is whether or not the activity creates market differentiation, the second dimension is whether or not the activity is critical for the continued functioning of the organization.

d

The following illustration is an example of a purpose alignment model.

FIGURE 4.6 Purpose Alignment Model

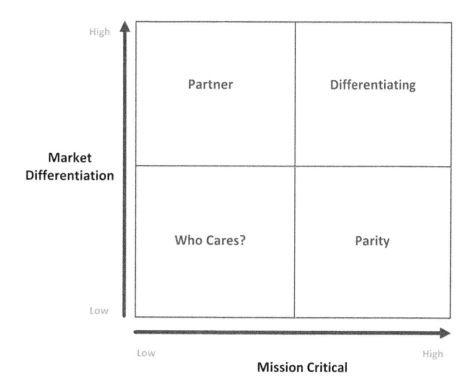

Elements

Differentiating Quadrant

Features, products, or services that both serve to differentiate the organization in the marketplace and are critical to the functioning of the company are part of the differentiating quadrant. These are the things in which the organization should be prepared to invest to offer something that is distinct from competitor offerings. A differentiating activity is one that might be used to advertise the company, that is difficult for competitors to match, or otherwise has significant strategic value, and a unique approach to these activities is likely to be needed.

Parity Quadrant

Things which are mission critical, but not market differentiating, fall into the parity quadrant. Many standard functions, such as finance, HR, payroll, and others fall into this quadrant for most organizations. Activities in this quadrant are important but they do not provide an advantage to the firm in relation to competitors and so adoption of best practices is generally sufficient.

Partner Quadrant

Activities that may have unique value to customers, but which are not critical to the functioning of the organization, fall into the partner quadrant. Even though these activities are important to customers or other stakeholders, the organization doesn't need to perform them to survive. That means that the organization is unlikely to have the resources to excel at these activities (as more mission-critical operations will take precedence), while a partner may perform them more effectively.

Who Cares? Quadrant

Activities which are neither mission-critical nor help to differentiate the organization in the marketplace fall into the who cares? quadrant. As these activities do not add customer value, and the organization can function without performing them, they are prime candidates to be eliminated and the resources reallocated to support more useful work.

Usage Considerations

The purpose alignment model is designed for use by for-profit organizations that face competition in the marketplace. Governmental organizations and no-profits may find that market differentiation is not a significant driver for their decisions. Stakeholder or member value, alignment with the organizational mission or delivery of social good may serve as an alternative to the market differentiation dimension. Even when different labels are used for the dimensions, the thinking behind the use if the model remains the same.

Secondly, the model provides guidance on whether something should be an area of strategic concern but does not provide any guidance on what strategies or decisions might be the correct ones.

Advantages

- One of the key advantages of this model is its simplicity. It can be taught to business sponsors and users in a couple of minutes so that they can critically assess an idea themselves rather than the business analyst do the analysis that may then be challenged.
- The model is easy to use in a facilitated collaborative environment.
- It can be applied all the way up and down the investment decision process. From strategic investment down to an individual feature in a system.
- It is fast and entire backlog can be analyzed in less than an hour.

d

Disadvantages

- It assumes positive intent in the business strategy. It does not incorporate "spoiler" behaviour by corporations.

4.6   The Delivery Framework

The Delivery Framework deals with the hows and the whens of the product. Effective delivery is supported by four underlying principles:

- Get Real Using Examples,
- Understand What is Doable,
- Stimulate Collaboration and Continuous Improvement, and
- Avoid Waste.

4.6.1   Get Real Using Examples

In agile approaches, in order to elicit and validate product needs business analysis practitioners use real customer examples to communicate with the team, including the customer. Real examples serve to bridge understanding of the customer's business and how they see the product serving a future state need. Analysis models can be concurrently developed and elaborated using these same examples. Models may be useful for the team but examples are more concrete for the customer. The techniques are used iteratively by alternating between examples and analysis models to explore multiple dimensions (for example, user role, user actions, data, and business rules) of a product need. This is a continuous practice that builds a shared team understanding of product needs useful for both planning and delivery. These techniques engage customers in requirements elicitation, analysis, and validation.

Examples and models should be at a level of granularity that is appropriate for the outcome you seek. When planning the product, models are used to set context and help the team and customer identify scope. These models are more abstract and provide a broad perspective of the problem domain. When delivering the product, the same model can be progressively elaborated and related examples are elicited and specified to launch into a deeper discussion of the dimensions. The examples can be used to derive acceptance criteria, help the developer design the solution, and provide a foundation for functional testing.

The following sections describe commonly used techniques for this principle:

- Behaviour Driven Development.

There are other techniques within the *Agile Extension to the BABOK®*
Guide, the *BABOK® Guide*, and other ad hoc techniques that can be utilized here as well.

.1 Behaviour Driven Development (BDD)

Purpose

An approach that enhances the communication between stakeholders and project team members by expressing product needs as concrete examples.

Description

Traditional business analysis techniques often involve creating analysis models. In addition to analysis models, agile techniques favour communication using examples which are more concrete for the customer. Many people are uncomfortable with abstractions and prefer to work with real examples.

Examples tend to be additive (growing in both clarity of the need and detail of the solution as the project progresses) and can form a specification. They can be used during agile planning and delivery work to help clarify and describe the requirements for the product being built. As models change, examples can be refined by building on previous examples. In agile, it is helpful to iterate between using examples and analysis models encouraging them to compliment each other. Progressive elaboration leads to richer exploration of multiple dimensions (for example, user role, user actions, data, and business rules) related to the example.

Supplementing product need discussions with examples creates a much more stable set of requirements than using a model alone. Examples feed smoothly into a behaviour/test driven development approach.

d

Elements

Examples

Examples may also be known as scenarios. Examples should not be artificial or made up. They should be real life business scenarios provided by the business users. Business analysis activities help to facilitate the discovery of the examples and ensure that the set of examples is comprehensive. Not all examples identified will necessarily be within the scope of a development effort.

Behaviour Driven Development

Behaviour driven development provides a simple grammar format that allows real scenarios to be filled in. This takes the form

- GIVEN <a context>
- WHEN <an event>
- THEN <an outcome>

Both GIVEN statements and multiple THEN outcomes for a single scenario could be compound conditions linked with AND statements. There is normally only one WHEN event that triggers the scenario.

For example, an ATM.

Scenario 1: Account has sufficient funds.

- **GIVEN**: I'm in credit
- **AND** the ATM has sufficient cash available
- **WHEN**: I request $20
- **THEN**: I receive $20
- **AND**: my account balance is reduced by $20
- **AND**: my card is returned

Scenario 2: Account has insufficient funds.

- **GIVEN**: I'm in overdrawn
- **AND** the ATM has sufficient cash available
- **WHEN**: I request $20
- **THEN**: I receive no money
- **AND**: my card is returned

Scenarios that are written in a behaviour driven development format specifying events, conditions, and actions are verifiable. They can serve as acceptance criteria for stories [See "Story Elaboration" on page 68] and serve as tests in support of Acceptance Test Driven Development (ATDD) that drive a common understanding of requirements and future product needs.

The terms BDD, ATDD, and Specification by Example tend to be used interchangeably in general use.

Testing

There are now a number of software products that will take examples in this format (but may have their own specific syntax and structure) and allow them to be easily converted into automated tests, thus enabling more agile delivery. With a comprehensive set of examples that can be executed as automated tests, business analysis and testing activities can be more tightly coupled.

Usage Considerations

BDD is a technique to make needs clear and is designed to improve communication and understanding across all members of a project team. Technical team members use the examples to understand what the product needs to do (development) and how to ensure that it does what is needed (testing). Customer representatives provide the examples and clarify their thinking by doing so. Business Analysis entails identifying the scenarios by asking many "what-if" question to expose additional scenarios and expressing these as additional examples.

Advantages

- BDD expresses customer needs in natural language, in a format that all team members should be able to easily understand.
- The structure of BDD lends towards acceptance test automation and supports the production of effective test cases.
- Tools exist to support the use of BDD in projects, and these provide additional metrics such as test case coverage or requirements.
- Scenarios can be easily prioritized which supports the iterative, incremental nature of agile projects.

Disadvantages

- It is possible to miss important scenarios unless there is someone who actively asks the "what if" and "what about" questions.
- Where business rules are very complex there could be too many scenarios to easily manage and track without tool support.

d

4.6.2   Understand What is Doable

As an agile project team plans for delivery, it is important to think about what is pragmatic and doable. The team must balance capacity and demand when they estimate the work to be done to deliver the product. Agile project teams continually review measures, such as team capacity, prior delivery cycle commitments and actuals, and velocity trends to adjust commitments on an on-going basis. This enables the team to question what can be delivered given their knowledge of the work-set, and to set appropriate expectations and make better estimates. Understanding what is doable occurs throughout any agile delivery cycle, such as release planning, work-ahead analysis, or whenever a team is pulling new backlog items for consideration in a product delivery cycle.

The entire team uses the following techniques as methods to identify and estimate units of work that are decomposed with business value in mind.

The following sections describe commonly used techniques for this principle:

- Relative Estimation,
- Planning Workshop, and
- Real Options.

There are other techniques within the *Agile Extension to the BABOK® Guide,* the *BABOK® Guide,* and other ad hoc techniques that can be utilized here as well.

.1   Relative Estimation

Purpose

Accurate estimation is critical to an agile team's productivity, reliability, and reputation. By being able to develop accurate estimates of cost, time, and effort, the agile development team has the ability to faithfully commit to a project or work effort.

Estimation is a team activity, and business analysis makes an important contribution by helping the team to better understand the components, characteristics, and complexity of the work.

Although estimates are not always visible in the final product, they do add significant value to an agile project. Providing credible estimates allows the project team to:

- determine cost and effort,
- establish the priorities of the project, and
- commit to a schedule.

On agile projects estimation is not restricted to being an initial planning activity, it is frequently undertaken early in the project during the initial story identification activities and estimates are refined and improved through constant feedback in the ongoing iteration planning activities.

Description

Estimation is discussed at length in the *BABOK® Guide* version 2.0 (9.10 Estimation). Here we build on the information in the *BABOK ® Guide* and summarize the relative estimation techniques that can be applied in the agile development environment.

Unique to agile approaches, estimating is progressive and occurs in alignment with iterations. No one expects early estimates to be as accurate as latter estimates. Improvement occurs over time as the teams build confidence in their capacity and capabilities.

In addition to the basic approach of estimating based on historical knowledge, agile estimators frequently apply a relative estimating model in which teams develop narratives (stories) that define user needs and benefits. These stories are analyzed by the team and numeric values are applied to each story (story points). Story points are normally used as an abstract measurement that provides a numeric value to a story; some teams and organizations use ideal developer days (IDDs) instead of relative points, although many commentators recommend against this approach.

A story point is a relative number assigned to each story that defines the estimated effort a team will have to apply to deliver the story. Story points are usually based on what the team knows about the story in four key areas:

- **Knowledge**: How much information does the team have?
- **Complexity**: How difficult is the implementation likely to be?
- **Size**: How big is the story? How long will it take?

d

- **Uncertainty**: What variables and unknown factors might impact the story?

The total number of story points delivered (to the agreed Definition of Done) within any given iteration is considered to be the team's velocity, or how much a team accomplished within the iteration. Over several iterations teams will have a better understanding of their actual velocity. This will allow them to make better informed estimates and commitments in subsequent iterations.

There are several ways to get started with story point estimation. The agile estimator can begin with

- an order of magnitude,
- a given set of resources and a fixed iteration, or
- a team based estimation of the time required for a sample of stories of different sizes, and then extrapolate from there to estimate the work that can likely be done in an iteration.

Usage Consideration

Advantages

- Relative estimation is a simple, reliable methodology that fits well with agile practices. It is highly adaptive and is likely to become increasingly accurate throughout successive iterations.
- The planning poker technique is a highly collaborative process that is based on consensus and will likely have a positive impact on development teams. It builds upon the wise counsel to "ask the team."

Disadvantages

- Relative estimates are based on historical data, and accuracy is dependent upon the similarity of new stories to stories previously delivered. If new stories differ radically from previous stories, it is possible that the accuracy of the estimate may decrease.
- The accuracy of velocity is dependent on the knowledge and experience of the development team working together. Any changes to team composition will impact velocity and therefore future estimates.
- Planning poker and relative estimation are not the only approaches to estimation and not all teams estimate their work before starting. There are other approaches which are not defined in detail here, and other metrics which are often tracked.

.2 Planning Workshop

Purpose

To enable the team to determine what value can be delivered over an agreed time period.

Typically there are two levels of planning workshop:

- one that covers the current release of the product and takes place prior to the start of iterations, and
- a more detailed workshop that focus on work to be done during the iteration.

Description

A planning workshop is executed when the team needs to arrive at a commitment to some set of functionality that they feel reasonably confident they can complete over an agreed time period.

The release planning workshop produces the release plan showing the intended sequence of delivery of user stories over the whole release.

The iteration planning workshop is performed at the beginning of each iteration, but may also occur whenever the team is near to completing their backlog of work or that backlog needs to be ordered. It is important that the team understands and focuses on the iteration objectives, the value associated with a particular MMF, business issues, story decomposition. Prior to the workshop, there is a pre-planning stage that involves analysis to get a reasonable gauge of the size, scope, and complexity of each backlog item that will be brought to the iteration planning workshop.

In agile approaches planning workshops need to be performed on a frequent and regular basis as the order in which work is meant to be performed is regularly altered and updated. This allows the team and customers to change the priorities of outstanding work to incorporate feedback or changing business needs.

In Kanban, the amount of work being performed by the team is limited by restricting the number of work items that can be in any workflow state, not based on iterations.

d

Elements

Estimated and Ordered Backlog

Typically based on user stories, it is the main input for the planning meeting.

Team Velocity

Prior velocity (throughput capacity of backlog items) is critical to enabling the team to schedule a realistic amount of work. When using Kanban, work-in-progress (WIP) limits will be used to manage this workload instead.

Iteration Goal or MMF Set

Many teams set an overall goal for the iteration to help guide the selection of features. This is a subset of the release goal. It is an objective that will be met through the implementation of the product backlog.

Requirement Selection

At the beginning of the meeting the iteration goal and the highest priority features are selected from the release plan by the product owner, product champion, or a customer based on business value and team velocity.

Non-Feature Selection

The backlog can also be composed of non-feature items (elements not related to a product increment) identified as necessary to achieve the iteration goal or deliver an MMF. For example, there can be bugs to be fixed, system or environment set up, research initiatives, management work items, or any other activity that add value to the project.

Task Planning

The team can choose to break the feature and non-feature items down into tasks. Tasks typically range in size from 4 hours to 2 days, with most tasks capable of being delivered within a day.

Usage Considerations

Advantages

- Customer, product owner, and development team can communicate and collaborate frequently about product vision and evolution.
- Customer and product owner can guide the project not just at the start but at every iteration.

- It's easier to understand, estimate, and plan the scope of small iterations instead of the scope of big releases.
- Plans can be changed in advance based on feedback from incremental delivery of working software.
- Iteration planning can facilitate visibility of the whole project and synchronization between multiple teams.

Disadvantages

- It is necessary to get all people together in order to avoid interruptions and rework, especially when working with distributed or concurrent teams.
- If the product is not well understood during the iteration planning workshop, it's possible to result in a suboptimal plan.

.3 Real Options

Purpose

An approach to help people know when to make decisions rather than how. The approach helps you understand whether you have a commitment or an option.

Description

The core concept behind real options is that you should delay making a decision or a commitment in a project until the last responsible moment, when the decision really needs to be made. The real option approach has three simple rules:

- options have value,
- options expire, and
- never commit early unless you know why.

The first and third rule tell you to avoid commitments and keep your options open. The second rule tells you to understand when an option expires so that you can actively manage whether you choose that option or let it lapse. As there is value in options, you should seek to extend the maturity of the options.

Real options address people's aversion to uncertainty by providing the conditions when a commitment should be made (the option expiry) rather than simply suggesting that they wait.

The most common usage of real options within agile projects is the way in which business investors chose which item to invest in next.

d

Traditionally, investors prioritize their requirements for an extended period of time. With real options, they only prioritize until the next investment decision point. On Scrum projects this occurs during the next sprint planning session. In Kanban, it occurs the next time capacity becomes available to work on something new.

Real options support agile approaches by allowing us to reduce the number of decisions we have to consider at any one time and delaying decisions about the detail of requirements as long as possible. This is achieved by treating the detail of requirements as options and the commitment point is when we elaborate in detail.

Elements

Options and Commitments

Real options forces you to identify whether you have options or not, and also forces you to identify the commitments you are making.

Examples of options include:

- A user story: an option to implement a piece of functionality. The option expires when the business need changes.
- A hotel reservation: an option to stay at the hotel. The option normally expires at 6 p.m. on the day of the stay at which point you are committed to paying for the hotel room.
- A business card: the option to contact the person who gives you the card. The option expires when the person changes contact details.

Options are things you can chose to do or not do. If you are committed to doing something and there is only one way, then you do not have options. Often there is a penalty associated with failing to meet a commitment.

Some examples of commitments include:

- Using the organization's standard software development language to build a product.
- Turning up to work on time. Failure to meet this commitment may result in termination of your contract of employment.
- Delivering items from the backlog that you have committed to deliver. Failure to meet this commitment will reduce trust and damage the team's reputation with customers.

Examples of things that are not options.

- Things you cannot do.
- Things you cannot afford.
- Things you cannot do in time.
- Things you cannot buy or sell.
- Things you do not have the tools for.

Options Expiry

Real options forces us to understand when our options expire or when we no longer have a choice. We have an option up to the expiry date but not after it. In financial options, the expiry date of the option is explicitly stated as a series of date/times. In real options, the expiry date is conditional.

Determination of when an option expires is the most important aspect of real options. Without this knowledge you are blind in your decision process. You either make decisions too soon or too late and you do not know which.

Example

You have a user story in the backlog which is due to be delivered in the next iteration. Prior to the iteration planning workshop you can elaborate the story to acceptance criteria to ensure there is sufficient understanding that the piece of the product can be built. Not doing the story elaboration could result in surprises when the work is started on the story which may result in the team being unable to meet their commitments for the current iteration.

As options have value, pushing the expiry date back adds value to your project and allows you more flexibility. The concept of the "last responsible moment" is key - making decisions too early restricts our choices, and deferring them too long can result in rework or other waste.

Right / Wrong / Uncertain

A rational decision process would order our preference as being right, then uncertain, and finally wrong. Observing people's behaviour though their preference is right, wrong, and then uncertain.

If you ask someone to defer a decision, they are faced with unbounded uncertainty and as a result they are likely to make a decision based on the information they have now. This emotional commitment then makes it harder to change the decision as further information arrives.

d

Real options suggests using bounded uncertainty. "Make the decision when..." Specify the conditions when the decision should be made.

Specifying the conditions when a commitment should be made allows the decision process to be managed. A senior manager can ask their assistant to monitor the conditions on his behalf.

Feature Injection

Feature injection is a collection of traditional business analysis techniques that have been combined to allow a business analyst to perform analysis in a fast and effective manner. This speed then allows investment commitments to be deferred because this reduces the length of time that analysis takes.

The speed of the process is due to following the Real Options process. The analysis starts with the output and then works back through the process to the inputs. It then considers how different examples affect the process.

There are three steps to the process:

1. Identify the business value which specifies the outputs/outcomes required from the system/process.

2. Inject the features that work out which processes and inputs are required to produce the outputs/outcomes.

3. Use models to identify all the examples that produce a different behaviour in the system/process.

Usage Considerations

Advantages

- Real Options simplify decision making by providing a simple set of principles to follow.
- Real Options make decision making fast as you only focus on the immediate decisions and defer prioritization until a later date when complexity is resolved.
- Real Options inform when, not how, to construct decisions, which makes them broadly applicable as an approach.
- Real Options optimize processes by forcing the consideration of the decision points and the information arrival process (when data arrives and whether it arrives before the decision).

Disadvantages

- Real Options can be counter-intuitive as they require us to analyze systems from the outputs to the inputs.
- Real Options are not a simple process to be followed by rote. They are a thinking tool that requires practice and study.

4.6.3 Stimulate Collaboration and Continuous Improvement

Agile approaches emphasize the importance of continual collaboration between members of the project community. It is the role of the business analyst to create an environment where all project stakeholders can contribute to the overall project value, ideally in face to face facilitated workshops. The reality for many projects is that they are distributed in terms of team, time, and geography. Facilitation skills, in conjunction with the techniques outlined in this section, enables collaboration for both local and distributed teams. The techniques in this section entail working together in groups to create a shared understanding. This collaborative point of view pervades an agile project, and is not limited to any specific technique.

One of the fundamental principles of all agile approaches is the need for continuous improvement, not just of the product under development but of the process used by the team to deliver the product. This is achieved through both structured and unstructured feedback on a continuous basis. For example, the retrospective is an opportunity for the team to examine their processes and product to identify opportunities for improvement. Healthy collaborative teams have the trust and safety necessary to transparently identify opportunities for improvement.

The following sections describe commonly used techniques for this principle:

- Collaborative Games and
- Retrospectives.

There are other techniques within the *Agile Extension to the BABOK® Guide*, the *BABOK® Guide*, and other ad hoc techniques that can be utilized here as well.

.1 Collaborative Games

Purpose

Collaborative games are not used strictly by agile teams, although they are prevalent in agile practices because they emphasize the concepts of teamwork and collaboration which are highly valued by agile practices. Collaborative games help a group of people promote a common understanding, gain insight into a problem, or inspire new ideas about solving a problem.

Description

Collaborative games refer to several structured techniques inspired by game play and designed to facilitate collaboration. Each game includes rules to keep participants focused on a specific objective. The games are used to help the participants share their knowledge and experience on a given topic, identify hidden assumptions, and explore that knowledge in ways that may not occur during the course of normal interactions. The shared experience of the collaborative game encourages people with different perspectives on a topic to work together to better understand an issue and develop a shared model of the problem or of potential solutions.

Collaborative games often benefit from the involvement of a neutral facilitator who helps the participants understand the rules of the game and helps to enforce them. The facilitator's job is to keep the game moving forward and to help ensure that all participants play a role.

Collaborative games also usually involve a strong visual or tactile element. Activities like moving sticky notes, scribbling on white boards, assembling things, or drawing pictures help overcome inhibitions, foster creative thinking, and think laterally.

Elements

Purpose

Games always have some defined purpose, typically to develop a better understanding of a problem or to stimulate creative solutions. The participants in the game need to understand that purpose, and the facilitator will help keep them moving toward it.

Process

Games also have a process or rules that they follow to keep the game moving toward its goal. Often, each step in the game is time limited. Games typically have at least three steps:

1. an opening step, where the participants get involved, learn the rules of the game, and start generating ideas,

2. the exploration step, where participants engage with one another and look for connections between their ideas, test those ideas, and experiment with new ones, and

3. a closing step, where the ideas are assessed and participants work out which ideas are likely to be the most useful and productive.

Outcome

Finally, at the end of a collaborative game, the facilitator and participants will work through the results of the game and determine any decisions or actions that need to be taken as a result of what the participants have learned.

Usage Considerations

It is not practical to elaborate on the many collaborative gaming techniques and their usage considerations in this document but the following examples may provide a starting point.

TABLE 4.5 Examples of Collaborative Games

Game	Description	Objective
Product Box	Participants construct a box for the product as if it was being sold in a retail store.	Used to help identify features of a product that help drive interest in the marketplace.
Affinity Map	Participants write down features on sticky notes, put them on a wall, and then move them close to other features that appear similar in some way.	Used to help identify related or similar features or themes.
Fishbowl	Participants are divided into two groups. One group of participants speak about a topic, while other participants listen intently and document their observations.	Used to identify hidden assumptions or perspectives.

Advantages

- May reveal hidden assumptions or differences of opinion.
- Encourages creative thinking by stimulating alternative mental processes.
- Challenges participants who are normally quiet or reserved to take a more active role in team activities.

Disadvantages

- The playful nature of the games may be perceived as silly and be uncomfortable for participants with reserved personalities or cultural norms.

- Games can be time consuming and may be perceived as unproductive especially if objectives or outcomes are unclear.
- Group participation can lead to a false sense of confidence in conclusions reached.

.2 Retrospectives

Purpose

The objective of a retrospective meeting is for a team to come together in order to reflect on what it has done well, what it could do better, and to reach agreement on how any improvements will be realized for both the product and the processes they use to create the product. Retrospectives are held at key milestones in the product life-cycle, normally at the end of every iteration, and at every release so that learnings can be quickly embedded in the processes and practices going forward.

Description

The retrospective provides an opportunity for all members of the team to reflect on the most recent deliveries. The retrospective should include the whole team. It is common for the retrospective to be split into two parts. The first part involving the whole team and the second part to discuss technical aspects of the project that only affect part of the team.

The retrospective should be focused on identifying issues with the process. It should identify process improvements, and not be personal in any sense. A key element of a retrospective is that the team feels safe to discuss any issue that concerns them.

It may be useful for retrospectives to be facilitated by a neutral facilitator rather than by a member of the team.

Where fixed iteration cycles are not being used, it is a good idea to schedule regular retrospectives so the team can examine their processes.

Elements

Preparation

The team prepares ideas from the recent iteration that may be analyzed in the retrospective.

Safety Check

The team must agree, together, to trust each other and to believe that every comment or suggestion is intended for the sole purpose of improving the team's performance.

Identify the Issues

There are many mechanisms to identify issues to discuss. One of the most common is for all team members to write up things that went well, things to improve, and things of interest on post-it notes. Colour coding the notes and applying them to a visual time-line assist in adding understanding to the emerging picture.

Choosing Future Actions

Once all the ideas have been discussed to the satisfaction of the team, the facilitator asks the team to decide which solutions/improvements they want to focus on next. The team then identifies which improvements will be addressed and assigns responsibility to an individual team member who ensures the solution/improvement is implemented.

Usage Considerations

Advantages

- An excellent way for the team to find a collective voice around opportunities for team improvement.

Disadvantages

- Team members may feel obliged to pretend that they trust each other, even though they do not.
- Retrospectives are only of value if the team acts upon the learning from the session to improve the process.
- Most ideas raised in the retrospective are known to at least one member of the team. A mature team should be addressing issues as they arise rather than batching them up to be handled in a retrospective.
- If issues raised in the retrospective are not addressed, there is a risk to team morale and motivation.

4.6.4   Avoid Waste

Agile approaches emphasize the delivery of working software to the customer. Business analysis work adds value by ensuring that the needs of the customer are understood and that the team delivers what

d

the customer really need. Any activity that does not contribute directly to this goal, or that the customer would not be willing to pay for, is waste.

Waste elimination is an issue that has been treated with great emphasis by the agile community. It is a mind-set originated from Lean as an effective way to increase the profitability of any business. Lean thinking considers a value stream as having two components:

- value adding activities, and
- muda (the Japanese word for waste).

The aim of Lean thinking is to remove the muda, or waste, from the value stream. Waste is further sub-divided into two components:

- those activities that have value but do not contribute to the final product directly, and
- those activities that do not add value at all.

The aim is to remove completely those activities that do not add value, and minimize those activities that do not contribute to the final product directly.

The following principles are helpful when working to identify waste in any business analysis activity:

- Avoid producing documentation before it is needed.
- Ensure commitments are met and there are no incomplete work items that adversely impact downstream activities.
- Avoid rework by making commitments as late as possible.
- Try to elicit, analyze, specify, and validate requirements with the same models.
- Analysis models should be as simple as possible. Do not include information that is not directly useful to a stakeholder.
- Work in close proximity to the customers and development team because unnecessary motion or work-a-rounds that substitute face-to-face conversations are also waste.
- Keep continuous attention to technical excellence. Quality defects (such as unclear requirements) result in rework and are one of the most undesirable forms of waste.

The following sections describe commonly used techniques for this principle:

- Lightweight Documentation.

There are other techniques within the *Agile Extension to the BABOK® Guide*, the *BABOK® Guide*, and other ad hoc techniques that can be utilized here as well.

.1 Lightweight Documentation

Purpose

Ensure that all documentation produced is intended to fulfill an impending need, has clear value for stakeholders, and does not create unnecessary overhead.

Description

Lightweight documentation is a principle that governs all documentation produced in an agile project. The team should aim to produce as little documentation as possible, all of which should be of value. The value of documentation should be explicit and clear. In a heavily legislated environment, such as health-care, compliance documentation has value and is not waste.

The context plays an important factor in the amount of documentation required. Some projects are mandated to produce documentation by external entities (for example, regulators). Documentation may also be needed to provide a long-term record of decisions reached by the team or functions implemented in the application. This documentation can be written after the software is developed, which ensures that it actually matches what the team delivered.

It is worth considering that if a document is valuable enough to be created, it is probably important enough to be automated so that it is part of the living code base. This consideration has led to the rise of automated acceptance testing and behaviour driven development that allows business analysts to work with quality assurance professionals to create executable specification in the form of examples.

This approach comes directly from the Agile Manifesto which says "Working software over extensive documentation". It is often misinterpreted as meaning no documentation. Instead, documentation should be barely sufficient to meet the needs of the team.

Usage Considerations

Advantages

- Reduces amount of time spent writing documentation.

d

- Reduces effort spent reading and reviewing documentation.
- Reduces number of drafts of documents.
- All reviewers can focus on key issues rather than extraneous details.
- Training (knowledge transfer) is done to suit each person rather than using the documentation.
- The documentation lives in the form of automated examples.

Disadvantages

- Producing lightweight documentation may cause conflict with groups who enforce corporate process standards.
- Some may misunderstand the principle as meaning no documentation.
- Some produce documentation that is not sufficient for an external entity.

d

Glossary

Acceptance Criteria

Requirements that must be met in order for a solution to be considered acceptable to key stakeholders. Acceptance criteria can refer to a requirement of any granularity, product, or delivery cycle.

Acceptance Test Driven Development (ATDD)

Involves writing one or more tests (or "customer tests") for a customer-centric feature, before the solution has been developed.

Agile Manifesto

A statement of the principles that underpin Agile Software Development. It was drafted from February 11th through 13th, 2001.

Agile Retrospective

Retrospectives are a variation of project retrospectives whereby the retrospective workshop is conducted at regular intervals throughout the delivery process, such as after each iteration and/or release.

Anti-pattern

A commonly used, yet ineffective, process or practice.

Backlog

A wish list of requests for features to be included in a product.

Backlog Item

An element that belongs to a backlog. It can be a feature, a bug fix, a document, or any other kind of artifact.

Behavior Driven Development (BDD)

A requirements elicitation and specification technique that enhances the communication between business users and the development team by using real examples.

Burndown Chart

Used to track the work remaining over time. Work remaining is the Y axis and time is the X axis. Also see Release Burndown Chart.

Business Value

In management, business value is an informal term that includes all forms of value that determine the health and well-being of the firm in the long-run. In agile development, business value is related to all deliverables that increase/protect revenue or reduce/avoid costs in a business.

Ceremonies

Controlled processes and documents that constitute events and outputs in any given approach. A high degree of ceremony frequently implies a high degree of control and traceability. Based on the just-in-time and just-enough model, agile projects generally have a lower degree of ceremony. Agile ceremonies include iteration planning, daily meetings, and retrospectives.

Class-Responsibility-Collaboration (CRC) Cards

A brainstorming tool used in the design of object-oriented software.

Daily Meeting

On each day of a iteration the team holds meetings. This meeting is used to set the priorities and context for the daily work.

Daily Scrum Meeting

See Daily Meeting.

Daily Standup

See Daily Meeting.

Delivery Team

A cross-functional team of skilled individuals who bring a variety of expertise to bear on the process of building a software product.

Elicitation

An activity within requirements development that identifies sources for requirements and then uses elicitation techniques (for example, interviews, prototypes, facilitated workshops, documentation studies) to gather requirements from those sources.

Epic

A piece of functionality that enables a user to achieve a clearly identified business objective. Epics are often large components of work that are decomposed into smaller stories and features. An epic helps tie features and stories back to a value-added business objective.

Feature

A discreet piece of functionality that has measurable business value. A feature is often delivered through the development of a number of user stories.

Iteration Burndown

See Product Burndown Chart.

Iteration Planning

The process of assigning user stories to particular iterations based on resources, effort, and priority.

Just-in-time Requirements

Requirements that define only what is needed for the current iteration and only to the level of detail required for the team to deliver the item.

Minimal Marketable Feature (MMF)

A coherent portion of functionality that is capable of returning value when released on its own. This could be an epic or a story, but is any level of detail that is minimally required to create a meaningful, valuable release for the customer.

Minimal Viable Feature (MVF)

Commonly used with new products. Also see Minimal Marketable Feature.

On-site Customers
The term used for the individual responsible for the relative priorities for the solution requirements in the Extreme Programming approach.

Persona
Fictional characters or archetypes that exemplify the way that typical users will interact with a product.

Plan-driven
A software development approach that follows an orderly series of sequential stages. Requirements are agreed upon, design is created, and then the code is developed and tested.

Product Backlog Item
A product backlog item (PBI, backlog item, or item) is a unit of work small enough to be completed by a team in one iteration.

Product Champion
See Product Owner.

Product Owner
The role on the team that represents the interests of all stakeholders, defines the features of the product, and prioritizes the product backlog.

Also referred to as product champion, business voice, and customer voice.

Product Roadmap
A long term/long range planning horizon features to deliver vision and value.

Progressive Elaboration
The act of continually defining requirements with successively greater levels of detail as needed through the life of the product or the feature within a product.

Rapid Application Development (RAD)
A generic term referring to any number of lighter-weight approaches, using fourth-generation languages and frameworks (such as web application frameworks), which accelerate the availability of working software.

Relative Estimation
A way of estimating work effort by identifying features/requirements with stories and then assigning story points to each story. The cumulative story points are the amount of effort to estimate the amount of effort required to deliver each story. The story points are then calculated against the team's velocity to create an estimate on how much the team can deliver in a particular iteration.

Release Planning
At the beginning of a project the team will create a high-level release plan. The team cannot possibly know everything up front so a detailed plan is not necessary. The release plan should address: the number and duration of the iterations, how many people or teams should be on this project, the number of releases, the value delivered in each release, the ship date for the releases.

Scrum Team

The team that builds the product that the customer is going to consume. The team in Scrum is cross-functional - it includes all the expertise necessary to deliver the potentially shippable product each sprint - and it is self-organizing, with a very high degree of autonomy and accountability.

Shippable Product Showcase

A fully tested unit of code which meets acceptance criteria that is delivered at the end of an iteration.

Service Level Agreements

Formal agreements that contract level of service and performance.

Solution Assessment and Validation

The set of tasks that are performed in order to ensure that solutions meet the business need and to facilitate their successful implementation. These activities may be performed to assess and validate business processes, organizational structures, outsourcing agreements, software applications, and any other component of the solution.

Sprint

An iteration of work during which an increment of product functionality is implemented.

Sprint Goal

A short description of what the sprint will attempt to achieve.

Sprint Retrospective

The main mechanism for taking the visibility that Scrum provides into areas of potential improvement, and turning it into results.

Standup Meeting

See Daily Meeting.

Story

See User Story.

Story Mapping

A technique to facilitate the understanding of product functionality, the flow of usage, and to assist with prioritizing product delivery (such as release planning). The output of the story mapping exercise is a product called a story map, which describes a workflow of user stories. Story maps may break user stories down into tasks for each process and may represent these tasks based on priority.

Task Board

The task board shows all the work the team is doing during an iteration. It is updated continuously throughout the iteration - if someone thinks of a new task they write a new card and puts it on the board. Either during or before the daily meeting, estimates are changed (up or down) and cards are moved around the board.

Team Velocity

The rate at which a team can consistently deliver software features per iteration. Typically, it can be estimated by viewing previous iterations, assuming the team composition. and iteration duration are kept constant. It can also be established on a iteration-by-iteration basis, using commitment-based planning.

Theory of Constraints

Developed by Dr. Eli Goldratt, the Theory of Constraints (TOC) holds that every system has at least one constraint limiting it. TOC's goal is to increase efficiencies by identifying and mitigating these constraints.

User Acceptance Criteria

Test cases that users employ to judge whether the delivered system is acceptable. Each acceptance test describes a set of system inputs and expected results.

User Story

A high-level, informal, short description of a solution capability that provides value to a stakeholder. A user story is typically one or two sentences long and provides the minimum information necessary to allow a developer to estimate the work required to implement it.

User Story Mapping

See Story Mapping.

Value driven development

A process used to prioritize requirements or backlog items based on business value.

Velocity

See Team Velocity.

Whole Team Testing

The concept embraced by many agile approaches where the entire project team is responsible for quality assurance and testing the code.

Index

Bibliography

The following works were referenced by contributors to the *Agile Extension to the BABOK® Guide*. In cases where multiple editions of a work were consulted, only the most recent edition is listed.

In addition to the works listed here, many other sources of information on business analysis were consulted by contributors and reviewers or otherwise or influenced the development of *The Agile Extension to the BABOK® Guide*, including articles, white papers, websites, blog postings, online forums, seminars, workshops, and conferences.

With only a very few exceptions, the ideas and concepts found in the *Agile Extension to the BABOK® Guide* were not created originally for or original to it. The *Agile Extension to the BABOK® Guide* is a synthesis of years of research into how agile development methodologies are utilized and methods that can be used to identify potential improvements. The works listed below, themselves build on the thoughts and research of many others.

Adlin, Tamara and John Pruitt. 2010. *The Essential Persona Lifecycle: Your Guide to Building and Using Personas*. Morgan Kaufmann.

Adzic, Gojko. 2009. *Bridging the Communication Gap: Specification by Example and Agile Acceptance Testing*. Neuri Limited.

Adzic, Gojko. 2011. *Specification by Example: How Successful Teams Deliver the Right Software*. Manning Publications.

Ambler, Scott. *Introduction to User Stories*. Agile Modelling. http://www.agilemodeling.com/artifacts/userStory.htm.

Anderson, David. 2010. *Kanban: Successful Evolutionary Change for Your Technology Business*. Blue Hole Press.

Arthur, Jay. 2006. *Lean Six Sigma De mystified: A Self-Teaching Guide*. McGraw-Hill Professional.

Berenbach, Brian, Daniel J. Paulish, Juergen Kazmeier, and Arnold Rudorfer. 2009. *Software & Systems Requirements Engineering: In Practice*. McGraw-Hill Osborne Media.

Chelimsky, David, Dave Astels, Bryan Helmkamp, and Dan North. 2010. *The RSpec Book: Behaviour Driven Development with Rspec, Cucumber, and Friends.* Pragmatic Bookshelf.

Cohn, Mike. 2004. *User Stories Applied: For Agile Software Development.* Addison-Wesley Professional.

Cohen, Mike. 2006. *Agile Estimating and Planning.* Prentice Hall.

Cooper, Alan. 2004. *The Inmates are Running the Asylum.* Sams - Pearson Education.

Cottmeyer, Mike and V. Lee Henson. 2009. *The Agile Business Analyst.* VersionOne, White Paper. http://www.agiledad.com/Documents/BAWhitepaperJune.pdf.

Courage, Catherine and Kathy Baxter. 2005. *Understanding Your Users: A Practical Guide to User Requirements Methods, Tools, and Techniques.* Elsevier Science and Technology Books, Inc.

Derby, Esther and Diana Larsen. 2006. *Agile Retrospectives: Making Good Teams Great.* Pragmatic Bookshelf.

DSDM Consortium. 2003. *DSDM: Business Focused Development, Second Edition.* Pearson Education.

Evers, Marc. September 23, 2009. *Working with User Story Mapping.* Dreamfeed: Marc's Weblog. http://blog.piecemealgrowth.net/working-with-user-story-mapping/.

Extreme Programming. September 28, 2009. *Extreme Programming: A Gentle Introduction.* http://www.extremeprogramming.org/index.html.

Goldratt, Eliyahu. 2004. *The Goal: A Process of Ongoing Improvement.* North River Press.

Gottesdiener, Ellen. 2002. *Requirements by Collaboration: Workshops to Define Needs.* Addison-Wesley Professional.

Gottesdiener, Ellen. 2005. *Software Requirements Memory Jogger.* Goal Q P C Inc.

Gottesdiener, Ellen. February 4, 2009. *The Agile Business Analyst: Eyes for Waste.* Modernanlyst.com. http://www.modernanalyst.com/Resources/Articles/tabid/115/articleType/ArticleView/articleId/811/The-Agile-Business-Analyst-Eyes-for-Waste.aspx.

Gottesdiener, Ellen and Mary Gorman. 2012. *Discover to Deliver: Agile Product Planning and Analysis.* EBG Consulting. Assets and resources available at http://www.discovertodeliver.com.

Gottesdiener, Ellen and Mary Gorman. *Better Software: May/June, 2013. Strengthen your Discovery Muscle.* EBG Consulting. http://www.ebgconsulting.com/Pubs/Articles/StrengthenYourDiscoveryMuscle(Gorman-Gottesdiener).pdf.

Gray, Dave, Sunni Brown, and James Macunafo. 2010. *Gamestorming: A Playbook for Innovators, Rulebreakers, and Changemakers.* O'Reilly Media.

Highsmith, Jim. 2009. Agile Project *Management: Creating Innovative Products (2nd Edition)*. Addison-Wesley Professional.

Hohmann, Luke. 2006. *Innovation Games: Creating Breakthrough Products Through Collaborative Play*. Addison-Wesley Professional.

IIBA (2009). *A Guide to the Business Analysis Body of Knowledge® (BABOK® Guide), Version 2*. International Institute of Business Analysis.

Jonasson, Hans. 2008. *Determining Project Requirements*. CRC Press.

Karol, Robin and Beebe Nelson. 2007. *New Product Development for Dummies*. John Wiley & Sons.

Kent, Stuart. June 30, 2004. *Storyboarding*. MSDN Blogs Stuart Kent's Blog. http://blogs.msdn.com/b/stuart_kent/archive/2004/06/30/169599.aspx.

Kerth, Norman. 2001. *Project Retrospectives: A Handbook for Team Reviews*. Dorset House.

Kim, W. Chan and Renee Mauborgne. 2005. *Blue Ocean Strategy*. Harvard Business Press.

King, James. December 28, 2010. *Estimation toolkit: Some useful techniques*. InfoQ.com. http://www.infoq.com/articles/estimation-toolkit.

Lean Enterprise Institute. *Principles of Lean*. http://www.lean.org/whatslean/principles.cfm.

Leffingwell, Dean. 2011. *Agile Software Requirements: Lean Requirements Practices for Teams, Programs, and the Enterprise*. Addison-Wesley Professional.

Lencionim Patrick. 2006. *Silos, Politics and Turf Wars: A Leadership Fable About Destroying the Barriers That Turn Colleagues Into Competitors*. Jossey-Bass.

Maassen, Olav and Chris Matts. June 2008. *Real Options underlie Agile Practices*. InfoQ.com. http://www.infoq.com/articles/real-options-enhance-agility.

Matts, Chris. October 29, 2003. *Zero Documentation*. The Agile Business Coach. http://abc.truemesh.com/archives/000103.html.

Matts, Chris. 2009. *Real Options at Agile 2009*. R.O.S.E. Comics. http://www.lulu.com/product/paperback/real-options-at-agile-2009/5949485.

Manifesto for Agile Software Development. http://agilemanifesto.org.

Merrifield, Ric, Jack Calhoun, Dennis Stevens. 2008. *The Next Revolution in Productivity*. Harvard Business Review.

Middleton, Peter and James Sutton. 2005. *Lean Software Strategies: Proven Techniques for Managers and Developers*. Productivity Press.

North, Dan. March 2006. *Introducing BDD*. DanNorth.net. http://dannorth.net/introducing-bdd/.

Patton, Jeff. *Building Better Products by Using User Story Mapping.* http://www.slideshare.net/nashjain/user-story-mapping.

Patton, Jeff. October 8, 2008. *The new user story backlog is a map.* AgileProductDesign.com. http://agileproductdesign.com/blog/the_new_backlog.html.

Patten, Jeff. February 26, 2010. *User Centred Design and Story Mapping.* InfoQ.com. http://www.infoq.com/interviews/patton-story-map.

Pixton, Pollyanna, Niel Nickolaisen, Todd Little, and Kent McDonald. 2009. *Stand Back and Deliver: Accelerating Business Agility.* Addison-Wesley Professional.

Pols, Andy and Chris Matts. 2004 *Five Business Value Commandments.* Agile Project Management Advisory Service Executive Update. Vol. 5, No.18. Cutter Consortium. http://cdn.pols.co.uk/papers/cutterbusinessvaluearticle.pdf.

Pyzdek, Thomas. 2003. *The Six Sigma Handbook, Revised and Expanded.* McGraw-Hill.

Rosenberg, Doug and Matt Stephens. 2007. *Use Case Driven Object Modeling with UML: Theory and Practice.* Apress.

Rother, Mike and John Shook. 1999. *Learning to See: Value-Stream Mapping to Create Value and Eliminate MUDA.* The Lean Enterprise Institute, Inc.

Sayer, Natalie J. and Bruce Williams. 2007. *Lean For Dummies.* John Wiley & Sons.

Schwaber, Ken. 2007. *Agile Project Management with Scrum.* Microsoft Press.

Schwaber, Ken; Sutherland, Jeff. 2010. *Scrum Guide.* Scrum.org. http://www.scrum.org/storage/scrumguides/Scrum%20Guide.pdf.

Shore, James. 2007. *The Art of Agile Development.* O'Reilly Media.

Sims, Chris. March 23, 2009. *Story Mapping Gives Context to User Stories.* InfoQ.com. http://www.infoq.com/news/2009/03/story-map.

Womack, and James P., and Daniel T. Jones. 2003. *Lean Thinking: Banish Waste and Create Wealth in Your Corporation, Revised and Update.* Free Press.

Wells, Don. 2009. *Iteration Planning.* XPProgramming.com. http://www.extremeprogramming.org/rules/iterationplanning.html.

Wynne, Matt, and Aslak Hellesøy. 2011. *The Cucumber Book: Behaviour Driven Development for Testers and Developers.* The Pragmatic Bookshelf.

Contributors

and The Agile Alliance® would like to thank the following contributors to the *Agile Extension to the BABOK® Guide*. Without their efforts and commitment the *Agile Extension to the BABOK®Guide* would not be possible.

- Kevin Brennan
- Susan Block
- David C. Cook
- Peter Gordon
- Steve Erlank
- Ellen Gottesdiener
- Shane Hastie

- Brian Hemker
- Marsha Hughes
- Chris Matts
- Ali Mazer
- David Morris
- Luiz Claudio Parzianello
- Carol Scalice

- Paul Stapleton, Editor
- Dennis Stevens
- Pascal Van Cauwenberghe

Reviewers

IIBA® and The Agile Alliance® would like to recognize and thank the many people who provided feedback through the public review of *Agile Extension to the BABOK® Guide*. Your feedback and guidance helped shape this Version 1 of *Agile Extension to the BABOK® Guide*.

International Institute of Business Analysis (IIBA)

International Institute of Business Analysis (IIBA) is an independent non-profit professional association dedicated to promoting the business analysis profession worldwide. As the global thought leader for business analysis, is dedicated to the development and maintenance of standards for the practice of business analysis and for the certification of practitioners. One of the main goals of the association is to help BAs develop their skills and advance their careers.

IIBA has created A Guide to the Business Analysis Body of Knowledge® (BABOK®) Guide, the collection of knowledge within the BA profession, reflecting the current generally accepted practices.

Membership in IIBA

Membership benefits include:

- The BABOK® Guide, the internationally recognized standard for the BA profession
- Online Library with access to 300 business books, a reference library at your fingertips
- BA Competency Model and the BA Competency Assessment to evaluate your BA skills
- Webinars delivered by industry leaders, providing current, relevant and actionable information
- Discounted exam fees for the Certification of Competency in Business Analysis™

(CCBA®) and Certified Business Analysis Professional™ (CBAP®) designations
- Eligibility to join a local Chapter
- Job search capabilities using the Career Centre

IIBA Certification

Certification of Competency in Business Analysis™ (CCBA®)

The CCBA® designation is a professional certification for BA practitioners who want to be recognized for their expertise and skills by earning formal recognition.

Certified Business Analysis Professional™ (CBAP®)

The CBAP® designation is a professional certification for individuals with extensive business analysis experience, the elite, senior members of the BA community.

For more information visit IIBA.org/Certification.

IIBA Chapters

Over 100 IIBA Chapters worldwide provide networking and professional development opportunities to business analysts at the local level through activities, meetings, and educational programs. Visit IIBA.org/Chapters.

For complete information visit IIBA.org.

The Agile Alliance

The Agile Alliance is a non-profit organization with global membership, committed to advancing Agile development principles and practices. Agile Alliance supports those who explore and apply Agile principles and practices in order to make the software industry more productive, humane and sustainable. We share our passion to deliver software better every day.

Agile methods have proven their effectiveness and are transforming the software industry. As agile methods evolve and extend, Agile Alliance fosters a community where organizations and individuals find ways to transition to and advance Agile practices, regardless of methodology.

The Agile Alliance website offers an information hub where members can access a wide variety of resources — an article library, videos, presentations, local user group listings and links to additional agile resources.

Agile Alliance organizes the largest, most diverse and comprehensive agile conferences each year. Conference participants learn from hundreds of sessions spanning the entire agile organization and life-cycle, make business connections, and converse with agile thought leaders, practitioners, and authors.

In addition to these major conferences, Agile Alliance provides financial and organizational support to scores of local, regional and special interest conferences and user groups worldwide.

The Agile Alliance operates on the principles of the Agile Manifesto.
http://www.agilemanifesto.org

The Agile Alliance web site is:
www.agilealliance.org.

CPSIA information can be obtained
at www.ICGtesting.com
Printed in the USA
BVOW07s1509240417
482044BV00015B/341/P

9 781927 584002